Endorsements

"Do you ever wonder what pastors do between Sundays? This book gives you the inside story: twenty-four stories selected from thirty-seven years behind-the-scenes with a small-town Montana pastor. You will laugh and you will cry, but you will not be bored. Dealing with God in people's lives is the stuff of high drama."
Eugene H Peterson, Translator of *The MESSAGE*

*"*Somewhere By Chicago *grabbed my attention immediately and held it until the very last word. In addition to wit, charm and gentle persuasion, the author shares wisdom from years of experience that is of enormous value to all readers. Quite simply, I love this book."*
Marilyn Meberg, WOMEN OF FAITH speaker and writer.

"Your chapter on 'Surprised by Pride' *is outstanding...describing the subtle yet toxic way that pride can infect a pastor. It is excellent in its diagnosis. Give us more."*
Marshall Shelley, editor of LEADERSHIP JOURNAL, a Christianity Today publication.

"After reading 'Marywood' *and* 'John Dowdall', *I am eager to read all of your reflections on ministry and life. I hope the sales go very well."*
Father Gary Reller, St. Anthony's Catholic Church, Missoula, Montana; Polson Colleague.

Somewhere By Chicago

JIM WALTERS

LAURA SCHULTZ TELLS ME
YOU HAVE WRITTEN A /
REMARKABLE BOOK !
MAY THESE STORIES ✗

MILES FINCH

MILES FINCH

miles004@centurytel.net

✗ INSPIRE YOU TO KEEP TELLING
THE OLD OLD STORY !

ISBN: 1-4392-3487-6
ISBN-13: 9781439234877
Library of Congress Control Number: 2009903054

Visit www.amazon.com or www.bonmotmedia.com or
www.booksurge.com to order additional copies.

Dedication

For Karen,
without whom I would not have
lasted two years in Polson

Table of Contents

Dedication

Acknowledgments

Introduction

Acknowledgements

My deep gratitude to:

- Eugene H. Peterson for his encouragement at every stage of this process.

- My wife for her indispensible support.

- The principle subjects for permission to tell their stories.

- Kimberly Crispeno, Kelsey Crispeno, Ann Vert, Pat and Mary Ellen Zoerner, John and Donna Briggs, John and Mary Ann Griggs, Polly and Ken Peterson, Jan Peterson, Anne Marie Heckt: these and many others helped keep me writing.

- Those who have endorsed the book.

- Leif Peterson who gave me writing and publishing guidance, and served as my editor.

- My publishing team for their expertise and help.

Introduction

You know exactly how I was made, bit by bit,
how I was sculpted from nothing into something. [1]

For one period of a year and a half, I wrote a page-long birthday letter to every person in our church, from the youngest to the oldest. I wrote 600 notes during that time, and in each I concentrated on affirming special and distinct things. At times I had to reflect awhile to isolate God's creative genius, but it was always there to be found.

The reactions were astounding. Children kept the small letter in a sock drawer with their other precious things. Or it might show up at a funeral on the memorial picture poster. One patrician lady, our fifty-five year old pianist, said she sat and cried for thirty minutes when she received the written portrait. She framed it for her wall. I kept hearing that people had never received a note like that. In a way it made me sad, for the letters were fairly quickly written, and I only concentrated on the most obvious of things.

Psalm 139 says that God casts each of us in a new mold. That is true for the iris in our eye, our spirit, our abilities, our experiences. As Eugene Peterson writes,

"The Bible makes it clear that every time there is a story of faith, it is completely original. God's creative genius is endless.... Each life is a fresh canvas on which he uses lines and colors, shades and lights, textures and proportions that he has never used before." [2]

The following stories highlight that stunning variety. Every person who entered our sanctuary for worship, every transient who plied us for funds, was unique. One of my goals is to give dignity to these people who might otherwise slip out of sight, to give these few more than a birthday note.

Chapter 1
THE CALL

Harvey was nothing if not pleasant, but one day he stormed into the classroom and slammed his textbooks down on his desk. He was rattled enough to resort to cliché.

"As far as I'm concerned, it's not what you know, it's who you know!"

I was tempted to agree. We were about to have another class at Fuller Theological Seminary on the "polity" or governing principles of our particular denomination. Only months from graduation, all six of us were anticipating the next chapter of our lives and were looking for jobs. All of us had expressed frustration. Harvey's search was petering out, and so was mine. What were the past three years and thousands of dollars about, if church politics ultimately determined our destiny?

Fuller Theological Seminary is inter-denominational, preparing pastors for at least one-hundred different denominations and groups. Its stated goal was to provide us students with the vocational tools we would use for the rest of our lives. We had bought expensive books by the score so that, wherever we served, we would have on-site sources of solid devotional, theological, intellectual and historical value. Each quarter we had stumbled in and out of three to five classes, and each class had a textbook written by a scholar with thirty years of experience.

We had taken classes on Homiletics and Hermeneutics, studied Greek and Hebrew all three years so we could dig deeply into the Bible's meaning. We'd worked a whole quarter on a five-page sermon, properly done, starting with the translation of the Hebrew, then proceeding through all the other 200 hoops necessary to give any congregation in America the Word of God, correctly, and with passion. A sermon they would love. Every week we were to prepare our sermon this carefully.

"It's not WHAT but WHO?" Our instructor jumped into the conversation. *"I'll agree with you, Harvey, if by the 'Who', you mean Jesus. Personally, I've never written a letter...either to be placed initially ... or to be moved. I have figured that the Lord knows both my address and my phone number, and if He wants me to move, He is perfectly able to arrange that on the other end."*

I had been writing letters to various places, and to my own Montana District. The superintendent from Montana had recently suggested that the church in Bozeman would be a perfect fit for me, but so far Bozeman hadn't called.

After the instructor's comment, I wasn't worried now. I stopped writing letters. God himself would place me! He would influence someone, somewhere, to dial my number and call me to their town. The search had suddenly become exciting, because I wasn't searching anymore. I was simply waiting to be found.

Then it happened.

"Hi, Miles, this is John Weaver. I was wondering: are you still saved?"

It was the pastor from Polson, Montana. Actually, I was a little put out with John at that moment, because he was the one that the church in Bozeman, the college town, my town, called for its pastor.

John had been in Polson for the previous ten years. Polson, on beautiful Flathead Lake, the largest fresh-water lake west of the Mississippi, flanked by the "Little Alps", the Mission Mountains of the Rocky Mountain front. It's like a town in Austria, and I was the one John wanted there. Before he had come to Polson, the church had gone through pastors like popcorn, one staying only for a week and a half. Another having an affair. Nine pastors in quick succession.

But John had broken the cycle. Now he was justifiably concerned that the next pastor be a stable replacement. So, as was his nature, he prayed about his successor, and my wife Karen and I came to mind. When John learned I was about to graduate, Karen and I became his recommendation to the Polson church board.

So it was that we flew to Montana, largely by a gift from a single board member. In the morning I preached my five-page sermon prepared over five months in my Hebrew class, the one that would make *anyone* lean ahead in his seat. I preached a sermon on prayer that night, and during the afternoon we toured the parsonage, where my pregnant wife immediately became nauseated by the colors in the various rooms.

While my green-gilled wife bravely chatted with the ladies, I talked with Keith Armstrong, Victor Miller, Francis Watne, Chester Paulson and Dean Sheneman (the church board), and they grilled me. Did I like to hunt? Wasn't I born on a farm? They did *not* ask if I liked to read and study for sermons, or ask about Fuller Seminary and if it were a good school. Nor about any skill in Greek and Hebrew. Nor about my grade-point average.

Well actually, yes, one did ask about my G.P.A. Keith, the chairman, and an engineer for the Mission Valley Irrigation Project, did want to know my grade point average and I was nervous about answering because it wasn't a 4.0. I didn't know it, but the fact that it wasn't quite that high pleased him because he believed straight-A students were prima donnas, and would be hard to please. They'd had enough guys that were hard to please.

Well, I passed, eventually. It was a Montana shoot-out with two other men, and the church heard all three before deciding. None of this present-day stuff where they discuss and think and interview forever and finally decide on one, so all candidates are spared the horrors of competitive comparison. Nope, it was three up, two down. The other two bit the dust and I just knew it was because of the marvelous sermon.

But I didn't pass for that reason. We found that out six months after we were ensconced in a newly-painted parsonage. One day JoAnne, our immediate neighbor and one of the church members, came over. JoAnne Klein, wife of Lyle. Both from a bar and saloon background: guitar-picking, country-music people all the way.

"Maybe I shouldn't tell you this Karen, but when Miles preached on his Sunday, none of us understood a single word he said. He was the worst preacher of the three, but when we prayed about your coming, we all just 'felt good' about it. We felt you were God's will somehow!"

So much for my Hebrew! So much for my five months of agonizing study on Psalm thirty-two! The big-game hunters and farmers and lumber-mill workers of Polson Assembly of God church weren't looking for Hebrew conjugations. They wanted someone to conjugate life.

Back at Fuller Seminary our class was nearing its conclusion. The visiting instructor wanted to know how our pastoral searches were going. John was accepted at a Bible College in Springfield, Missouri. Gary was going to a church in the state of Washington. Harvey hadn't found a church yet. (And he never would in our denomination. He decided to join another community-church association; he did find a pastorate there.) And me?

"I'm going to Polson, Montana!"

What my pastor/instructor said in response was totally unexpected. The more I reflected on it, the more it clashed with what he had said before, that God Himself would always place me or move me. That first word seemed so true, God's word to me, and it had stuck.

But now I was hearing a replay of the conversation that Peter and Jesus had on their last trip into Jerusalem. On that occasion, Peter had just given Jesus one of the most magnificent pronouncements ever made by a man, *"You are the Christ, the son of the living God!"* [3] Then he immediately turned around and became a mouthpiece for Satan himself, trying to dissuade Jesus from accepting God's will, from accepting the Cross and self-sacrifice. *"Never, Lord! This shall never happen to you!"* [4]

"Miles, where did you say? Montana? You're going to MONTANA? Where's that? Somewhere by Chicago? You're making a big mistake! If you want a large church someday, the way to do it is first get on the staff of a large church, and when another large church desires a pastor, they'll come around and ask, 'Hey, how's that Finch? Is he a good man? Should we consider him?' That's the way it happens, Miles. You go to Montana, and you'll get buried there. Nobody will ever hear of you again!"

It happens. It happens still. People can be the very mouthpiece of God, and then turn right around and be the mouthpiece of Satan. We simply must learn to distinguish which is which, and that day I had to decide which of my pastor's statements came from God.

A shudder went through me as he said I might get "buried" up there in Montana. I feared he could very well be right. I knew it didn't make any political or career sense to head for a small Montana town, especially when I had the opportunity to be on his church staff in Los Angeles. Was he expecting me to approach him for a staff position? We had talked about that a year earlier, and perhaps this was behind his strong feeling and statement. These thoughts flickered in my mind, but inside I also said to myself with surprising resolve:

"Yes, Montana! God did call me to Montana, Mister, in accordance with your own previous confident statement that God knows my phone number. And God did call that number. John Weaver did hear from the Lord. And I just might get buried there the rest of my ministerial life. What you say might happen. But I still feel this is God's will."

It happened. It happens still. He was right. I did get "buried" there. I served that church for thirty-seven years to the very day. Only a few other towns ever called. And my pastor/friend/teacher in Los Angeles? My Peter?

He soon left his large church with rumors of moral failure … with both his secretary … and his daughter-in-law. I have thought many times since:

"Some recommendation his would have been!"

6

Chapter 2
DESCENT INTO HELPLESSNESS

When Karen and I began our ministry in Polson, this white settlement on the Salish-Kootenai Indian reservation, we had twenty-nine bona-fide members. By working real hard for three years, I got it down to thirteen!

I joke about that now, but it isn't really a joke, because that's what happened. The church was on the edge of losing its designation as a "sovereign assembly" and reverting back to a "district-dependent" church.

Of course, the descent didn't happen overnight. Everyone close to it, though, noticed where we were headed, and it was embarrassing. I didn't think this was supposed to happen to a graduate from Fuller Seminary. The congregation was confused, too, because they thought they had sensed the will of God.

Things did get desperate, and not just for us as a family. Financially, the church was in deeper and deeper trouble, and Keith Armstrong, for years the chairman of the church board, finally had to write a letter to the congregation about the sorry state of the church's financial affairs. It was a woebegone letter, so much so I couldn't bear to keep it.

What in the world happened? It didn't work like this in my student parish up the road in Bigfork. Finances there had been very good. People had come...the church had grown. That was, after all, why I'd decided to proceed in the ministry...it seemed then like a pastoral calling was a "go". It sure didn't look like it now.

But there were reasons for the descent, of course, and many of them traced right back to me. The most glaring was deeply interior, something actually praised in our whole society and lauded nationally on July 4th. Americans love the concept of independence, and Montanans even more so. The hills and valleys, the farms and little towns here are chock full of independent, redneck, obstinate cusses, who don't like being dependent on others, or don't like feeling any sense of helplessness. Even though times get tough, there is a pride in leaning into the struggle and working a little bit harder. Somehow we'll squeak by.

It's not just Montana, really. Or America! It's world-wide. It's all of history! Self-sufficiency, I see now, is close to the center point of sin. When Satan approached the original pair in Eden, the argument winning his case was that they wouldn't have to confer anymore with that old Duffer who came into the garden each evening to "...*discuss things.*" Didn't they see He was just a control freak, a micro-manager? Just a little bite, and they wouldn't need Him to spell out what to do next, or what was right here, wrong there. It wouldn't be that maddening "yes" now, and "no" later, to the very same thing. They wouldn't have to be dependent on anyone anymore, even God. They could run their own lives, thanks. They could be self-sufficient. Is anything more appealing?

That's what had crept back into my own spirit. I walked around and did my thing as if it were a foregone conclusion that all would go well. Truth be told, I didn't really need to pray, because I didn't need God's help. This wasn't spoken out loud of course, even to myself, especially to myself. But this attitude was deep in my core. It was the buried germ of sin and self-sufficiency that doomed us to such a dismal beginning.

After all, I had a good education. I had a Master's degree from one of America's best seminaries. I had a B.A. from Seattle Pacific University in Psychology. At SPU I had received an "A" in Biblical Preaching from Dr. Ralph G. Turnbull, pastor of First Presbyterian Church in Seattle. (He had even pressured me to become Presbyterian.) Dr. Clarence Roddy, my Homiletics professor at Fuller, seemed to like me. Once I was chosen to be substitute Church-School teacher for Dr. David Allan Hubbard (the seminary's president) at the large Lake Avenue Congregational Church in Pasadena. I had acceptable intelligence, sharp ideas, wasn't the ugliest man in the lineup, and had the prettiest wife in town. What could possibly go wrong? Well, a lot could go wrong, and it did!

It was mostly because I wasn't praying, really praying. Praying because I needed God's help and God's blessing. Oh, yes, I prayed. But only as the Pharisees and Sadducees did…in places and ways that people could see. Pastors are supposed to pray, of course, especially at public things like church, and on special occasions. I could wax eloquent at those moments and say the right things, but did I really mean them? More importantly, did I pray much out of sight? On my own? Because I knew I needed God's help? No. Not much. Like Adam and Eve, I didn't need God's help anymore. I didn't want to confer with Him very often. My sinful nature had flared, and my Montana conditioning had returned in force. I was getting along fine, thanks.

What a colossal mistake, and what a toll it took!

All of us were mystified. Nothing, but *nothing* was happening. People weren't being "saved". The finances had tanked, in some minds the example *par excellent* of God's not blessing a ministry. Nothing unusual or miraculous was happening, such as apparent healings. I noticed that everywhere Jesus traveled the summary was that he taught in power, preached in power, and healed all manner of diseases among the people. Happening with me? No way.

I was descending into complete and obvious helplessness. After Keith wrote his unabashed appeal to the congregation, pathetically begging them to help, I started to wake up. Suddenly, after three years of free fall, I became frightened. If this trend continued, I was not only out of this particular church...I was out of the ministry. What other congregation would ever want me? Or, why would I even want to continue myself? God was obviously not working with me (the real key for all Christians, not just leaders), and He was the One I was actually supposed to be working for, so what did this misery spell? Failure, that's what.

So...I began to pray. I began to need God again. Like I had in Bigfork in my student pastorate! I began to search the Scripture for some answers, and one day I noticed the first words Jesus spoke in his Sermon on the Mount, the first Beatitude, the very first item in this discourse which has been called the Magna Charta of the Christian Faith. *"Blessed are the poor in spirit. THEIRS is the kingdom of heaven."* [5]

At first I wanted to say, *"Yeah, yeah, I know that!"*

But the Spirit of God within seemed to answer, *"Hey, Bud, hold it right here. Something is buried here that you really need."*

So, I dug deeper. I got out my Greek texts and helps and looked up the definition of the word "poor" as it was used here. It was...eye-opening. Revolutionary, actually! It doesn't mean *somewhat* poor, but still able to make it. It means flat-on-your-back poor. _Helpless poor!_

Helpless? I didn't like that word, or that feeling. Nobody likes that word or that feeling. Value helplessness? Who wants to feel helpless, un-self-sufficient, dependent, or absolutely worthless? Here, in the first words of Jesus' most major sermon, he holds up total dependence and stark helplessness as the default attitude, the number-one goal of every person in the Kingdom of God.

This is the door in. This is the key to having God work with us. This is the valid Kingdom reason churches grow and finances improve, and teaching and preaching and faith bring forth results. Someone is totally depending on God and not themselves. Not their education. Not their appearance. Not their humor. Not their friendliness, or their ability to lead worship, or speak thoughtful ideas. They need God's help in everything or they are sunk. They know it, and they show it. It seemed my *descent* could rather be called an *ascent*.

Ascent into helplessness? I choked on the idea that this was a good thing, the best thing that had ever happened to me, that I should desire this attitude for a continuous reality.

That's not good self-image talk.

That's not good psychological principle.

That is totally opposite to human reasoning.

And it *feels* absolutely awful.

But as I reflected and prayed further, I saw this as the key into the Kingdom of God. Furthermore, if you reverse each of the subsequent Beatitudes, you have the principles of the Kingdom of Darkness. So it's no wonder the first principle felt so strange.

For another example, reverse the Ten Commandments and you will see how the world is really run. When people don't want our country to subscribe to those marvelous guidelines, what do they want instead? That we live by their opposites?

You would think, wouldn't you, that I would suddenly be on my knees twenty-four hours a day, crying out desperately to God for help. Well, it didn't work that way. When we are so steeped in independence and so conditioned to go it alone, it takes time and sometimes tiny steps to change the pattern. At least that's what happened with me.

I did one simple thing that must have reversed the tide: I called a weekly prayer meeting for the men of the church and asked them to gather on Saturday nights for just one hour of sincere, dependent prayer for the good of the church.

I was disappointed the first Saturday when I was the only one who showed up. The next Saturday I was more frustrated. The third Saturday I was more discouraged still. And the fourth Saturday...well, that was the only night I ever felt like swearing in a prayer meeting.

For the last thirty minutes I wrote out the resignation scorcher that I would read the next morning. I wouldn't preach. I would just read my statement about their slobbish Christianity, and walk out.

Fortunately, I didn't follow through. I did have another dry-as-dust sermon ready to go, and that was plan B. Plan A was still my idea, though, as I trudged slowly up the stairs from the church basement toward the "platform," as we still call the chancel. My thoughts (God?) quietly said,

"Miles, of course you were the only one praying this month. That's what a leader is. A leader is always the first one to do something. Isn't that the way it works?"

So I preached my sermon and spit out my sand. One more Sunday like all the rest.

But it wasn't really. Not at all! Something wonderful had happened after my prayer meeting the night before, the one main thing I had prayed for all month. For the first thirty minutes the previous night, I had prayed to God *"with strong cries and tears"* for that one main thing, and God had heard! My ministry and the church turned around on a dime.

Chapter 3
GARY AND SHIRLEY

One of the things that could help you understand our early circumstances is that I test out to be extremely impulsive. I wasn't to see this for about fifteen years until the Christian author, Norman Wright, administered the Taylor-Johnson Temperament Analysis Test (TJTA) to a group of us. That tool refracts a personality into nine variables.

The last variable shows a person's test score on the column of Regulated (100) to Impulsive (0). My wife predictably scored eighty-eight (88). I scored eight (8). The test instructions told me that when I fell in the "white" like that, I was not Excellent, nor Acceptable, or Improvement-Desirable. I was Improvement-*Urgent.*

Further, I was told that the prognosis for a person like this is horrible. Even my impulses at improvement would be just that... impulses. Not much hope for me, if this were true. Norman Wright, knowing me a little by then, didn't think it was an accurate measurement, but my wife thought the test hit the nail right on the head. The authors were telling me,

"Look, Guy, of all the people we have tested since the 1940's, you fall in the category of the most impulsive of all. You have to change. You have to challenge something in yourself."

I grudgingly admitted they were right. This was a good explanation of much of our home tension. On my way to church on any given day, I would probably swing into three or four restaurants, hit a couple of businesses to chat with the owner, stop a few people on the street. As a Pentecostal, I had the ultimate rationalization for all of this impulsiveness: I was *"...being guided by the Spirit!"* I really don't have to tell you that my wife was often highly anxious...like...every day I walked out the door.

"What if someone dies, or goes to the hospital, Miles, and I have to find you? I won't know where to look."

Of course I see today the difficulty posed by my frequent urges. I have worked against them for years, with progress, but impulsiveness still sneaks up and bites me occasionally.

Do remember, though, that the legitimate leading of God's Spirit can look much like irresponsible impulsiveness. You have heard many stories by conservative people, non-Pentecostals, even non-Christians, who have sometimes obeyed a "hunch" and then seen God do something unusual.

I hope you can see, too, how slavishly following some lock-step precedent can keep God penned up, and inflict boredom, inefficiency, or a straitjacket on a person or a church. God, you know, occasionally likes to play 'Fruit-basket Upset.' Just when we get our lives all neat and tidy like a Parcheesi game, God bumps the board and scatters our marbles. Couldn't we legitimately expect a few more surprises than we see in our highly-controlled lives?

And so it was, in my vagabond wanderings, I came across Gary and Shirley at the second-hand store. They were both funny, and we laughed a lot. He was a red-haired European multi-ethnic and she an attractive Norwegian. Couple their personal liveliness with a store full of bargains to buy, and you know *some* spirit would often guide me there. We became good friends.

I was even able to interest them in an evening Bible study. They and one other couple agreed to go through the entire book of Romans, where the "Romans Road" to salvation is embedded. What a great opportunity to lead them to Christ! It was a cinch, a done deal!

Yeah! Sure! We went through the whole book of Romans. I tried my best, but neither of the couples made any commitment. The wife of the other man was Presbyterian, and very committed, so she was more than okay. But she was also going to another church. Gary and Shirley were skittish about both our church and any radical changes. Shirley had some Pentecostal influence in her past, but Gary had grown up a Methodist.

One specific fact about Gary was a conundrum to me: as a teenager he had gone to a Methodist Bible camp where one night they were making resolves and throwing pinecones in the campfire. He suddenly had a strong desire to become a pastor. Gary was a person of principle, a man of intelligence, and admitted being desirous of more spiritually. So why was he holding back?

One reason: he was at least borderline alcoholic. The night of his high school graduation, Gary tasted his first beer. Instantly he fell in love with the stuff. He was thirty-five now and for years, on binges, he had stacked the cans to the ceiling and couldn't control himself. He needed God's help, not just mine. I needed God's help, too, but just couldn't see it. I had met Gary and Shirley in the earliest days of my pastorate, so for three years we socialized, and talked, and argued, and laughed and sized each other up, and went through Romans. But nothing happened.

This is where things stood the month of the men's prayer meetings. Gary was the focus of my prayers that month. He was my test case for the first Beatitude, the advocacy of helpless prayer. I told the Lord at the beginning of that month that I was going to take my hands completely off Gary for this experiment. I wouldn't visit. I wouldn't call. I wouldn't drop by. I would just pray. If anything happened, it would definitely be God's doing.

On the fourth Saturday night I really prayed for Gary. Time was running out; I was desperate (a good synonym for helpless). Flat on my back now, just as Jesus cried out in prayer "...*with strong cries and tears*," [6] so did I that night. You could have easily heard me had you walked by the church. That was for the first thirty minutes. The last thirty minutes my anger at the church men took over, and I wrote my resignation.

Gary got drunk while I was praying. Shirley kicked him out of the house. It was winter. The only place he could go was to his old red-and-white Ford pickup parked behind their home. (They were by now the first local managers of the "Town Pump", a franchise which blankets Montana these days. They lived in a double-wide trailer on the premises.) It was there in the pickup that God finally showed up. Gary, deep into helplessness himself, cried out,

"*GOD, PLEASE!* <u>*SAVE*</u> *ME!*"

Facts have verified it since: he was suddenly, totally, stone-cold sober. Miraculously, the drunk was gone. That drunk and *that* drunk! Gary was instantly changed, and though many alcoholics would challenge the story, he never had difficulty with it again.

Into the house he went to tell Shirley, and they both wondered and watched all that Sunday as they tried to grasp the event that had taken place.

Meanwhile, I was over at the Polson Assembly of God church, grinding through a gritty sermon and perspiring through another Sunday.

After the evening service, my wife herself suggested an impulsive thing. Not knowing of my struggle the night before, or about my near-miss with resignation, not knowing about Gary's rough and wonderful night...she suggested that we take the kids and *go visit Gary and Shirley.* I couldn't remember her ever wanting to do anything after church at night but put the kids to bed and collapse. I was delighted, of course, so I quickly accepted and we went to the Town Pump because I did need to fill the car with gas.

They invited us in, and we had a conversation with the predictable good laughs which didn't go anywhere spiritually. As we drove away my wife was reflective.

"Gary seemed different tonight. I think something has happened! Maybe we should go back and ask."

You had to know Karen those days to grasp how strange her impulsive suggestions were. (She, too, could be guided by the Spirit, but her guidance usually came after prayer...as it was that night. She had been praying for this couple, too, you can be sure. Probably it was her prayers that turned our low tide, but don't tell her.)

"Gary, we just had to come back. You seemed different tonight! Did something happen we don't know about?"

So he told his story, and how unusual it was that he sobered up so fast. How different he seemed! He radiated the impression that he had been "born again". For a confirmation to him, he had prayed an additional prayer that night...that I would come storming into the trailer (in the middle of the night), grab his pipe and smash it against the fireplace, thus dealing with his nicotine habit too... neatly taking care of both addictions in one fell swoop.

Interestingly, I had awakened in the night, and had the idea of getting up to drive around town, but I choked off the urge, reasoning that it was probably related to my plans to resign and my subliminal uneasiness over that. Sometimes even Pentecostals feel they are getting too, well, *Pentecostal.*

That's how my ministry reversed in its disastrous course, literally overnight. Gary's conversion was compelling and genuine. They started coming to our church, which gave everyone some encouragement at long last. I saw that God really would work with me if I would flow with Him, would sincerely pray, and depend, and understand that supernatural things will only happen if we live the very first Beatitude. The things that should happen in a church ... people coming to Christ and being really changed ... people being healed in any human quadrant ... GOD has to do those things. He's the only one who knows where our buttons are, and He's the only one that can push them. If He's not working with us, we are sunk.

Another unusual incident is connected with Gary and Shirley. One night I had a vivid dream in full color. In it I walked into a garage in Sandpoint, Idaho, and there was Gary and Shirley's 1962 green Pontiac convertible, buckled and smashed by a head-on collision. Its white top was stretched toward the ceiling. In my dream I walked up to a mechanic and asked what happened to the people in the car.

"Oh, they were taken to a hospital in Spokane!"

That was the dream. I awoke with a start. The next day I just could not shake the dream or an urge to call them about any trip plans.

"Shirley, I feel ridiculous asking this, but are you planning any trip soon?"

"As a matter of fact, we are. We're leaving right after work to go to Portland."

"What road were you planning to take?"

"Well, we thought we'd try something different and go Highway Two."

"So you'd go through Sandpoint!"

Of course I then related my vivid dream and my subsequent concern.

"Hmmm! That's interesting," she mused. *"You know, all night I worked on a new dress for Angela, and while I was ironing it, I couldn't shake the thought, 'This is Angela's funeral dress.'"*

They didn't take the trip.

I wish I could say that our two families had been close all these years, but that's where things in the ministry and life don't always follow our preferences.

A later addition to our church was a man who considered himself our resident perceiver. He thought he had the gift of discernment, when it was really a gift of "suspicion" or a desire to control. One disastrous evening he went by Gary's and Shirley's and roto-rooted her with hurtful "insights." It was not at all his place to do this but there was no calling it back.

Gary had already been thinking of changing churches for over a year, since they lived near the bigger town of Kalispell. After our unwise member reamed her out, Shirley agreed with Gary and they chose to attend another church. I was so glad they didn't give up on Christ or on the faith, but their leaving was a deep, deep loss to Karen and me over the succeeding years. We did maintain a distant contact, however, and late in Shirley's life we reconnected.

Life in the ministry is always up and down, ebb and flow, and such disappointments are "occupational hazards". I want to be honest in these stories, so I am going to give an accurate picture of what ministry is like. In a church, people are "all over the map", and you have to learn to live with incompleteness, bloated egos, stupidity, surprises, interruptions and reverses – with *being-saved sinners* – or you just can't take it.

Someone said, *"A pastor should always mow his own lawn, because then he can see one thing he did that week!"*

I took that advice. Mowing my acre every week was a necessity for my sanity. A common social greeting to me has been,

"How's it going?"

I have often answered,

"That's hard to say. At any one moment it seems that something has me encouraged, something else has me concerned, and yet another thing has me scared to death!"

Are you a Christian idealist? Welcome to the real church!

Chapter 4
ALAN THE TRUCKER

Not long after Gary was converted in his pickup, we started an evening Bible study at the home of Chuck and Phyllis Klein. Chuck was the Chet Atkins (famous guitarist) of the whole area, and Phyllis was born Assembly of God in every cell.

I'll never forget one particular night. Gary and Shirley, Chuck and Phyllis, Karen and I, and Dean and Bonnie Allred were joined by Alan and Flossie Jones. Alan was a trucker, driving one of Dean's 18-wheeler logging trucks. Many in our church were employed by PlumCreek Lumber, a main stabilizing economic factor of our area for all of my thirty-seven years in Polson.

While the women were fixing munchies, Gary and Dean became quite animated in a conversation about "being born again". You already know of Gary's experience.

Dean was one of the original people I inherited, along with Bonnie. Dean had a dramatic Christian beginning and has always been a sharp and steady man in the church. Of Mormon background, he detested legalism and loved the relaxation found in grace. No man in town was more admired by his business and personal friends. Dean had the heart of a servant, doing practical things all year long. Bonnie? She already shines like the sun in God's kingdom! Her significant service, rock-solid commitment, and great love for Christ still blesses all aspects of our church's life. These two, Dean and Bonnie, have been stabilizing parishioners in our congregation before, during, and since our tenure.

As Gary and Dean enthused at the Bible Study about the moment when Christ changed them, and what came afterward, Alan listened with wide eyes. Finally he spoke.

"Hold it. Hold it right there. Wait a minute. I don't understand what you guys are talking about with this 'born again' stuff. All my life I have felt warm toward Christ and warm toward the church, but I can never remember anything like what you describe now. This is a mystery to me."

So we all chimed in and tried to explain the unexplainable. Conversion, from my perspective of a lifetime now, is a many-sided splendor. Too many want to force it into their little definition, and want all experiences to be the same as theirs. And our denomination has stressed the dramatic and the spontaneous.

Personally, from my constant inter-denominational interaction in college, seminary, and through my whole ministry, I have come to listen for variety in the Christian experience called "being born again". For many Christians it has been a 'table call' and not an 'altar call'. They have grown up around Christian tables hungrily watching their hot cereal get cold while the Bible was read and morning prayers were said. Still, somewhere in their youth or childhood, the miracle of commitment and conversion happened.

But Alan wasn't satisfied with his previous understanding and experience. Shirley was right on when she said,

"*Alan, it's like when you and Flossie were married. You made a commitment to her in front of everyone, and you obviously meant it. Your part in becoming a Christian is very similar.*"

My added thought was this:

"*It's just a prayer away. It is so simple that many people stumble over the obvious. It involves a commitment to Christ, that, come hell or high water, you are His forever. Like Shirley just said, when you were married, in front of a bunch of people you followed a preacher phrase by phrase in a vow of commitment. And that was going to be good for a lifetime, right? It didn't matter that you didn't make up the statement. It didn't matter that you repeated words someone else composed. That commitment changed your life!*"

Nothing happened for a few minutes. The conversation got bumped onto some other topic. But great resolve was simmering in Alan's mind and heart. Finally, he couldn't take it any longer:

"*Hold it! Hold it right there! I want to do it. I want to give myself to Christ right now!*"

So I said,

"*Terrific, Alan! All you need to do is follow me in a simple prayer. I've worked out the prayer carefully, basing it on important Scriptures, and you can trust me. Just follow me phrase by phrase.*"

I started out,

"*Dear Heavenly Father…*"

But Alan didn't follow my instructions. Instead he practically yelled,

"*JESUS!*"

Then he started to wail. It was such a cry of anguish that all the rest of us could do was snap open our eyes and gawk. We looked at one another uneasily because none of us knew what was going on. Had he lost it? No, he had found it.

As suddenly as the anguish came, so did the joy. His cries and tears turned, as we listened, to one of the most satisfying cries of joy I've ever heard. We HEARD the guy being "born again". We were witnesses to a resurrection, the most important kind humans can experience: resurrection in the spirit.

In distinction to what I've said about 'table calls' and 'quiet conversions', I've never participated in a more dramatic moment than Alan's second birth. Somewhere in Alan God pushed the right button, and all the gears of eternal life spun into action. Alan's spiritual engine roared to life.

It took a fair amount of time for him to calm down enough to explain, with not a little embarrassment on his part, how good he felt and what he thought happened to him. And of course that was the main reason we were there that night anyway. When Alan and Flossie had agreed to come to the study, all of us were hoping and praying this very thing would happen. So with tears in our own eyes now, we listened to him enthuse and cry, babble a bit and explain.

"You know something," he said when he had calmed down, *"I think I've not only been 'saved'. I think I've been healed. I've never cried since my folks divorced when I was a teenager.* (He was now in his 30's.) *I think something's happened to that part of me, too."*

That was in 1970 or so. In 2005 I was privileged to conduct the funeral for Hildur, his mother-in-law. There were Alan and Flossie, and their kids, and their grandkids, all solid in their faith. Alan sauntered over to me during the memorial meal and with tears in his eyes said,

"You know, Miles. It all started that night!"

Yes, it all started that long-ago night. *"JESUS!"* A one-word prayer. But it was the only word he really needed to pray. I thought again of the Scripture, *"Whosoever shall call on the name of the Lord shall be saved!"*[7] I just never realized it could be that literal.

Chapter 5

THE WRITING ON
THE WALL

I was sitting in my study staring at the wall, dreaming of a house on the other side of the block. Ray Biggerstaff, an old gentleman of eighty, was nearing death and I had been visiting him for a while before his illness. I was fascinated by his house: it was a three-story building, one of the first framed buildings of Polson. He said it had, at one time, been the town's hospital.

I saw opportunity! The first floor could be at least two, and perhaps three apartments, the second floor a three-bedroom home, and the top floor an "A" frame with a stoop overlooking the town and the Mission Mountains. Ray would sell it to me for $12,500. He would throw in all the antiques (every room was loaded) for $3000 more.

Of course, the house could be my own home, too, but with a salary then (1968) of $4400 per year, plus a wife and two children, it seemed foolish to purchase something like that.

On my mind that day was another minister in town, a wonderful colleague who had a lovely wife and five outstanding children. College expenses would be significant someday. He had found thirty acres of land near Finley Point – an exclusive area – for $30,000. The land was loaded with huge old-growth trees (pickles) that could be sold, plus Flathead Lake frontage on one side of it, and a house with ten bedrooms.

Sandy had discovered the opportunity while calling on the owner who had, single-handedly, built that huge house as a loving gift to his wife. It could have been left as a tourist attraction because every room was parquet, meaning the man had cut up thousands of pieces of different types of woods and placed them artistically on every ceiling, wall, and floor. Try to imagine: ten bedrooms done like that, in addition to all the other rooms. A lifetime of passion and love was invested there.

But the wife died and the old man's main reason to live was gone, so he sealed off the kitchen with a tarp and lived in that one room, drinking cherry wine non-stop. Out of his deep gratitude when Sandy led him to Christ, the transformed gentleman sold everything to my friend.

After the deal was done, and the old gentleman had died, Sandy decided to remodel the house for a foster home. The first step was to rip out those thousands of painstakingly placed pieces of parquet. I was there the day they burned the pile.

There was also a big barn on the place full of antiques and a meadow fronting Highway 35, ideal for sixteen house-trailer rental spaces. Another area was good for an overnight campground. Sandy was developing those possibilities, putting in underground utilities.

"So if he can, why can't I? I need to be investing for my children's college as well!"

Thus went my thoughts that Saturday morning when I should have been working on my sermon. At that precise moment, my eyes focused on a Scripture I had placed on my study wall, the one used in my ordination service in 1967:

"But you, O Man of God, FLEE these things. Follow instead after righteousness, godliness, faith, love, patience, meekness...." [8]

What I was to flee, at base, was the desire to be rich...that can prompt many other temptations and foolish lusts *"...which while some coveted after, they have erred from the faith, and pierced themselves through with many sorrows."* [9]

In addition to fleeing the desires that cluster around wealth, and following after the right things, this Scripture urged me to fight the good fight of faith and get a grasp on eternal life, for it was that to which I was called. Finally, I was to affirm that *godliness with contentment* was great gain. At my ordination, the sermon built on this scripture by Reverend Erwin Rohde was so stirring that I went home and made the wall hanging with ceramic letters.

That Saturday morning I saw why. I needed to be called back to my primary purpose for being in Polson, called back to my reason for being in the ministry at all. Even if my pay was low and my work was hard, I needed to forget about Sandy's fantastic deal, forget the Biggerstaff house with its antiques and possible apartments. My long-term assignment was to trust God for college money and future needs. And that Saturday I was to get back to sermon preparation.

Sandy couldn't continue his leveraging of assets, and debts piled up because of the way things went with his projects. The dreams didn't synchromesh as well or as quickly as they were planned, so the Bishop of his denomination ordered him to sell everything and move to another town. I disagreed strongly with that decision, as did scores of other people. In commendable obedience to his Bishop's leadership, though, Sandy sold it all and went other places to minister.

His leaving was tragic for Polson because he was an amazing speaker, motivator and administrator. He had the gift of illustrating truth better than most pastors I have heard before or since. A solid evangelical, he knew how to lead people of all ages to Christ, and his church was growing at an impressive rate. If he had been allowed to work through his financial issues, he would have grown a strong and large congregation. He was a marvelous man of God!

O how I've missed you, Sandy. You, who asked me to teach you ping-pong, and then promptly blew me off the table. You, who forgot you had a funeral and went fishing instead. You, who went with me to the Billy Graham School of Evangelism in Portland, and then came home and actually applied what you learned. You who once said *"Shame on you!"* in such a kind way that a man promptly came to Christ. Sandy, I still miss you!

In my study that Saturday I couldn't take my eyes from the words on the wall. Suddenly I was back in Great Falls, Montana, listening again to Reverend Rohde and realizing the dangers that can come with money. It didn't matter any longer that Sandy could legitimately continue with his real estate development, or that other pastors had better pay packages. I could bless my colleagues on their way while avoiding something dangerous for me.

An incident before my senior year at Seattle Pacific University came back to mind. I had stayed in Seattle that summer, feeling

I needed to take a bigger step toward personal independence and financial responsibility. In the years before, I had gone back home and pumped gas at Bigfork Texaco. But that summer in Seattle I took three jobs to make money for my fourth year of college.

First, I cleaned a church so large it had eleven pianos. Next, I worked scraping and painting the exterior windows on a large apartment house on Queen Anne Hill. From my painter's scaffold I overlooked the space needle, the Seattle Center, and downtown Seattle.

For my third job, I sold Fuller Brush products door-to-door in an ethnic and poor district of Seattle. Big mistake! This job sapped all the money I made on the first two! I ended up at summer's end with a car full of spider spray and sachet that customers ordered but couldn't pay for, so here I was, heading home at the end of summer, and my dire straits hit me. I prayed with strong intensity:

"Lord, I need $1000 before school starts, and I don't have any idea where it will come from. But I'm only going to tell You! Not my folks. Not Karen. And certainly not her dad!" (Karen and I were engaged.)

The very next day Karen's father asked,

"You're going to need some money next year, aren't you?"

"Yes, I guess I will," I replied sheepishly. (Nuts! I was trapped!)

"How much? About $1000?"

"As a matter of fact, I was thinking about it just last night, and that is the figure I came up with!"

He didn't know how frightened I had become that summer about my ability to provide for a family, for *his* daughter. If I couldn't meet my own needs, with three jobs, how did I dare think I could provide for a wife and children? He was thinking this, too, but didn't need to say it: it was written all over his face.

Eventually, God gave me a "word" of encouragement:

"I have been young and now am old; yet I have not seen the righteous forsaken, or his children begging bread. He is ever giving liberally and lending, and his children become a blessing." [10]

On the strength of that promise alone, I mustered the courage to get married and trust God.

How He provided for one particular need of our family has always prompted gratitude. I grew up on a ranch in eastern Montana. Beef was not to eat: it was to sell. We had hundreds of deer munching nightly in our grain fields, so we lived on venison. Yes, we poached. Before the age of fifteen, with our .30-30 Winchester, I twice brought down deer at 300 yards, each running away from me. One shot, at night, was taken in the beam of a spotlight. Talk about luck!

Karen's father, however, owned Meats Supply in Kalispell, a wholesale/retail meat store, and her family ate the choicest cuts of domestic beef. My folks decried those prices, so until I was married I ate venison. Understandably, after I proposed, I prayed:

"Lord, that she's the daughter of this particular meat merchant frightens me. Please help us in life with that item."

In our early marriage…through the last of college…through our first pastorate…through seminary…God answered that prayer in many special ways. But it was during the bulk of life, for our whole time in Polson, that He answered my frantic plea in a spectacular manner. Within the first week after our arrival, a farmer in the church unloaded an entire beef in front of our freezer…cut, wrapped, labeled and free! And get this: that farmer soon quit our church, because he felt I couldn't preach worth sour beans, or because he felt I got the wrong education, or for some other reason.

His family still liked me (or Karen), and the man was incredibly generous, so the supply of meat never ended. For all but a very short period in my tenure we always had beef. And pork. And chickens. From a farmer who wished I would go somewhere else. It doesn't compute, aside from the fact that God answers prayers of young husbands-to-be.

During my ministry my income level was usually below what was projected as average on most charts. It remained adequate, though, because the Lord made it such. God gave Karen and me the grace to trust Him. We were to look to the Lord and not to the board. We were to live within our income. We were not to be hang-dog about it or look penurious.

When we have needed something beyond that, money has come from unexpected places. Both of my children graduated from Seattle Pacific University and from Princeton Theological Seminary, each owing only about $5000 at the end of seminary. Since then, they have been financially healthy on their own.

"*...I have not seen his children begging bread.*"

Back once again to the writing on the wall: that ordination text became, again and again, my ordination *test*. Was I still on track with the Lord or not? I could find out by checking what I was presently "fleeing" and what I was "following". Those ceramic letters, "*But you, O Man of God, flee these things...and follow these...*" stayed there for years.

Chapter 6
FRANK LEFTHAND
AND
PIERRE BROWN BADGER

Polson is a white settlement on an Indian reservation. The Salish-Kootenai tribe of Indians originally roamed hundreds of miles in each direction from the beautiful five valleys in Western Montana: the Mission, Bitterroot, Jocko, Ravalli and Flathead. The tribe extended its territories or travels up into Canada. They are known as the Flathead Indians.

For most of the reservation's history there has been an uneasy truce between the white settlers and the tribe. In the last third of a century the tribe has been aggressive in claiming the rights given it in the Hellgate Treaty of July 16, 1855. In that document the tribe was assigned this area for its Reservation, with Polson being in the Northern segment.

Litigation is very common and ongoing about such things as who owns the water on and under the Reservation. Newcomers were given fee-simple deeds to the land they bought, and so there is often tension in the towns. The names of the Native people are as colorful as the mountains and the countryside: Weaselhead, Old Horn, Lefthand; even the name, "Shoots-'em-In-The-Foot."

Part of my parish assignment, then, was to relate to Native-Americans in the area. A Blackfoot Indian from over the mountains at Browning came to my office one day seeking money to get home, claiming that some Kootenai thugs were bent on killing him. The animosity between the Blackfoot Tribe and the Flathead Indians was intense in frontier days, and the residue of the conflict continues in covert ways. This young Blackfoot had to get back to Browning. Would I buy some gas?

Anglo-Saxon transients came wanting money too. One lifted $400 of my own money while I was out of the office. I had given him a shovel to trim the grass along the sidewalk while I went to lunch. Sure, I locked the door, but Jerry, a regular summertime visitor as he came through on his annual vacation to Canada, could pick locks and he had seen the money (from my Inspirational Bookrack's sales) being sorted on my desk. Wow. That probably financed his whole trip.

Native-Americans occasionally sought financial assistance, and their requests were inventive. It was hard at times to sort fact from fiction. I usually tried to share Christ in some manner and they listened. Genuine contact was made at times, and over the years I had many delightful and memorable relationships with this segment of my parish.

One such person was Pierre Brown Badger. He, with his wife and son, lived just two houses from us on 12th Avenue West. My son and his son often played together in our back yard on our merry-go-round, in our tree house or sandbox.

But Pierre was a fighter. Though he would easily pass for a "white" outside, he was fiercely "red" inside. Being of mixed heritage, he seemed to have difficulty claiming his Native-American identity with both groups. He had a delightful personality when sober or not angry, but put him in a bar with some firewater inside, which was often, and his dominant makeup would quickly flare. He wore an insulated vest so he could fight quickly without constricting sleeves.

Pierre seemed to make a Christian beginning but the old habits were strong! I recall one night when I made the rounds of the bars in Polson and the nearby town of Ronan trying to find him and help him away from his old life.

But I never quite made it with Pierre. The years of conditioning, the ingrained reverse-discrimination, the victim mentality that fueled his hate, the family and Native-American pressure against the change I represented, eventually won out. When coupled with Pierre's own sinful nature, his subterranean hostility was often inflamed.

One evening he went into a bar in the neighboring town of Ronan. As usual, he got into an incendiary conversation, this time with the bartender. Pierre decided to slam the guy and rounded the bar. The bartender didn't *"...take to this too hot,"* so he pulled a pistol from somewhere and aimed at Pierre.

"Don't come one step closer or I'll shoot!"

Pierre took another step. The bartender fired!

"If you're going to be like that," said Pierre, *"I'll take my business somewhere else!"*

So he went across Main Street to another bar. Sitting on his stool he started to itch on his stomach. Finally he reached in his shirt to scratch, and his stomach was *wet!* Not surprisingly, pulling out his hand revealed a lot of blood.

"I've been SHOT!" he shouted.

So they took him to the hospital in Polson thirteen miles away.

At the hospital they discovered that the bullet had gone all the way through Pierre, missing everything important on its trajectory through Indian country. All they did was put one bandaid on the entry wound, another on the exit wound, gave him some antibiotics, and put him to bed. Pierre didn't like the arrangement.

"Why are you putting me to bed?" he demanded. *"I'm all right."*

So he got up, dressed, and took off down the street toward another bar. About a block away, he collapsed from his trauma and loss of blood.

"Back to bed, Pierre," said the nurse. *"And you stay there this time!"*

I recall one particular visit to his home in my hope for his conversion. While we were talking I couldn't get my eyes off a picture on the wall, painted on black velvet. It was a picture of Satan. In an oval around his leering face, his main enticements were depicted: a glass of wine, a naked woman, a dripping needle, a deck of cards, a stack of money and...a couple more things. The picture highlighted for me the stark contrast between a life following Satan and one following Christ. There are so many more good things to do than bad things. Satan, however, has a Ph. D. in marketing.

The picture was over-simplified, of course. Our enemy uses far more temptations than the things on Pierre's picture. He uses the objects painted there, yes, but also malls and big-box stores, tons of car lots, $500,000 home theaters (a house near ours has exactly that), internet porn and games, and many other things. To me as a pastor, this barrage of competition and evil at times seemed insurmountable. I reminded myself of Luther's words that, *"...though this world with devils filled / should threaten to undo us / We shall not fear for God has willed / His truth to triumph through us."* Thankfully, the Gospel works with Native-Americans as well as anyone, and our church always had several.

For instance, there was Frank Lefthand. I didn't have a hand in Frank's conversion, but through his middle and last years I helped sustain him in Christ. Frank was a large man and had been on a professional baseball team. Alcohol derailed that promising career, but the Lord and Frank arm-wrestled his demon to the mat. All the years he was in our church I never heard of his having a drink. He had "recovered" or was in a state of "recovering". Interestingly, he didn't attend AA.

He was in church faithfully and couldn't have been more different than Pierre. Frank was what the locals labeled an "apple"...red outside, white inside. Well, that's not quite right: both sides claimed him. He was arguably the favorite Native-American in town.

A single man, he loved all the local sports programs and was at most events. He would travel the state as a supporter of Polson's athletic teams. Involved in the local theatre company, he did a wonderful job in the play, "One Flew over the Cuckoo's Nest." He worked at a local furniture store, and it was through the owners, Jerry and Pat Fisher, that Frank discovered our church. If Frank wasn't sick or at a sports event out of town, he was in church sitting up there on the "shelf" (in the balcony), front and center. It did rankle me, though, that he liked my wife's speaking over mine. He told me that quite frankly (pun intended).

One day Frank was sitting on a public bench on Main Street in front of the Flathead Courier, our local newspaper office. Suddenly his scalp began to itch, so he took off his baseball cap and absent-mindedly held it upside down over the sidewalk, with his elbow resting on his knee. As he scratched his head languidly with his other hand, a tourist happened to stroll by. Seeing this pathetic victim of white supremacy and domination reduced to ignominious begging, the passerby dropped a dollar in the hat.

Frank loved that story because it was so far from the truth. It was rare that Frank asked for financial help, at least from the church. He lived in a dark basement apartment and managed to live on his meager income. For years he worked at Harbor Light Furniture delivering furniture and doing odd jobs.

Only once did Frank come to our home with serious spiritual intent. The conversation was interesting for two reasons: first, in his usual delightful manner, he would have long pauses between his comments. He would say,

"Um, Miles...I've been thinkin'..."

Then it would seem five minutes before he would actually share what his thought was, but both Karen and I knew we shouldn't push him. The other reason the conversation was interesting was the subject material: cremation or burial? He was for burial.

He died while driving our church van. Fortunately he sensed something wrong and pulled to the curb and stopped. His passenger/friend was able to shut off the engine and summon help, but it was too late. Frank was gone.

I conducted the funeral at Koostehah Hall, the main Kootenai Tribal Hall in the tiny town of Elmo. Hundreds of people were at the wake all night long. Christian hymn after hymn was sung in the Native language. The music was plaintive and poignant, to say the least. I followed the English translations as they sang.

The next day I spoke to about 400 people, and had the perfect opportunity to share Christ with mostly tribal people. I tried to make the gospel clear and appealing, but their faces seemed impassive and hard to read. Perhaps more was received than I perceived.

But we tried, Frank and I. I guess that's all we could do.

Chapter 7
CONVERSATION BY THE CEMETERY

When I accepted this church, even though I was trying to be noble, career ambition was strong. I was furtively watching Missoula, seventy-five miles to the south, which had the University of Montana, plus one of our larger churches in the state. I could see that as a place I could stay for a lifetime.

Incredibly, the large church did come "open" three different times in my first seven years of ministry. On the third go-around I was hoping the church board there would notice a certain seminary-trained young man in a nearby town and give him an interview. Get that far, and maybe I had a chance.

But why should they even glance my direction? I had struggled to keep both the church and my family alive during the first two Missoula pastoral changes. Why would they want me, with that kind of record? By the third Missoula transition, things were more promising in Polson. It was not dramatic enough for others to notice, however, so again there was no phone call, not even a whisper of interest.

After this third missed opportunity I was in a real funk. More than ever my little village seemed a dead-end destination. The plywood mill had just closed, taking yet more jobs out of town, and some of our people. The promised new college for the tribe didn't materialize, and there were junk cars on vacant lots, nestled in weeds up to their windshields. The stores on Main Street were shabby and unappealing.

Right then the Polson Chamber of Commerce had a promotional campaign going entitled, "Proud of Polson!" I was so unhappy I wrote an article for the Flathead Courier entitled, *"Proud of Polson? Why?"* I had just visited Disneyland where they swept up all cigarette butts immediately and our dirty main street gutters depressed me.

In this dark, uncomplimentary mood I drove by the cemetery. Suddenly some strong thoughts came, and I recognized the voice of the Lord:

"Miles, is this graveyard good enough for you?"

"Um, why do you ask?"

"Oh, it's just pretty clear that you are grumpy and out of sorts, and I take it you are unhappy about Missoula overlooking you again. But what if I want you to live here and die here? Would that be okay? A Chicago surgeon named Teal liked Polson well enough that he lived and died here, and he is planted just to your left. So... is this cemetery good enough for you?"

"Give me a week to think about it!"

In a week I gave my reply that, yes, it would be okay. I would stop wanting another place. I would cheerfully commit myself to this dumpy little knapweed-infested town with its endless potholes and junk cars, and gladly commit to this wild array of people and own them as "family". I would give my work my best effort. I would pray. I would still try to reach this community for the Kingdom. *Cheerfully* and *gladly* was stretching it, but yes, I would stay.

It was time to reaffirm the value in God's eyes of the small and the insignificant. The pull toward prominence is a big occupational hazard for many pastors. We can affirm God's humble designs for the people of Scripture, like those for Jesus himself when he was called to Bethlehem, Nazareth, and Galilee. But then we turn right around and lust for the spotlight. Carlo Carretto speaks directly to the issue:

"Astonishing! The Son of God – who, more than anyone else, was free to choose what he would – chose not only a mother and a people, but also a social position. And he wanted to be a wage earner. That Jesus had voluntarily lost himself in an obscure Middle Eastern village; annihilated himself in the daily monotony of thirty years' rough, miserable work; separated himself from the society that 'counts'; and died in total anonymity." [11]

God therefore calls many of his people to serve others with an entirely different mental wave-length. Isn't that odd and rather debilitating? Well, no, if we choose as our models the Apostles Paul and Peter. Look at what God did with these two earliest examples of the Christian life: He sent the bumbling and uneducated fisherman, Peter, to the theological eggheads of Jerusalem, and he sent the well-trained theologian, Paul, to barbarians and gentile playboys.

Some university students once asked me why I went into the ministry. What constituted "a call"? I replied that at base, a Christian calling of any kind is as mysterious as is a call to the sea. Why seamen have chosen their kind of life has always been baffling to me. Would anyone in their right mind want to float for days in the doldrums on some ocean, or pitch up and down on frightening waves, or look at seascapes forever? Why would they want the cramped quarters and the strained relationships of lonely and frustrated fellow seafarers? I would never want that. But the call to ministry, seen from many perspectives, is just as incomprehensible.

My fifth year of college I worked at Boeing in Seattle. A supervisor in Research and Development discouraged my going into the ministry and wanted me in his division. He had persuaded three other men to abandon their call to be pastors and hoped he could me as well. During the conversation he also labeled the Holy Spirit as *"...stupid!"* This sounded dangerously like the unforgivable sin, and for me red flags popped up everywhere.

Though I saw the creative and career appeal of that particular division of Boeing, I couldn't shake my call or the picture of what had happened a day before the supervisor's offer. A man had retired that day and was rushing home to his retirement party. He died the instant he hit the exit turnstile. I filed through the next lane while they were trying to resuscitate him.

"That could happen to me, too," I thought as Dave, the cynical supervisor, spoke. So I declined the offer.

Another thought that defined my sense of call was a statement from the Apostle Paul. He once said that he was only going through the prisons, exiles and rancor in his life because *"Christ's love has moved me to such extremes. His love has the first and last word in everything we do."* [12]

Jesus said to pray for "laborers" to go into the fields white with harvest. Why pray for others to do it, if I was not willing?

My call was first glimpsed while I was still a teen. I recall staring at the stars above my parents' Flathead Lake cherry orchard and contemplating space and the reach of eternity. The greatness of God and the honor of serving Him flooded my thoughts, while the materialistic gains of earth seemed short-sighted. Why live for money only to quickly come to the age of sixty-five and find myself sitting on a pile of gold (maybe) and colon cancer? Paul the Apostle said:

"Compared to what's coming, living conditions around here seem like a stopover in an unfurnished shack, and we're tired of it. We've been given a glimpse of the real thing, our true home; our resurrection bodies! The Spirit of God whets our appetite by giving us a taste of what's ahead. He puts a little of heaven in our hearts so that we'll never settle for less... But neither exile nor homecoming is the main thing. Cheerfully pleasing God is the main thing, and that's what we aim to do, regardless of our conditions." [13]

One time a delightful woman came to speak for Sandy, my previously-mentioned local colleague. Her name was Mary Webster, and I remember one of her stories. She said she once bent over a lowly little morning-glory flower and asked it the question,

"Little morning glory, why have you struggled so, pushing through this sod and why have you braved the elements as you have?"

The little flower happily replied, *"To bloom for God, for just one day!"*

All of us should be willing to do the same. God's will for most of us is to grow in obscurity *"... and waste (our) fragrance on the desert air."* [14] Why should it really matter if we live and die only seen by the Lord?

Mary Webster illustrated her point in her own person. She had come to Polson from upper-central Montana. Ever been there? Talk about a windy, lonely place! But a beautiful and aromatic person named Mary was there, and her fragrance wasted? Not at all, for God watched her study and read and think and pray and love and serve there, and He was pleased!

What happened after the conversation by the cemetery? Did things remain the same in our church? No. Progress started immediately, seemingly initiated by a financial seminar. A young CPA from Gresham, Oregon, had wondered what the Bible said about money. He noticed much, of course, but particularly that we don't really give any *offerings* until we are giving above 10%.

"Anything below that is robbing God Himself," he added, *"and that's a very dumb thing to do. Tithe is the rent on life! If you watch how you spend the 90% of which God gives you more control, the 10% will be there easily. God will see to that."*

He shared another concept which was hand-sewn for our church, a principle buried in God's blessing on Abraham: *"I will bless those who bless you, Abraham; and conversely, I'll curse those who curse you."* [15] Our CPA expanded his thought:

"It follows that God implies here: 'I will be stingy with those who are stingy with you.' If God calls someone to serve in His Kingdom, then He really notices how others treat him/her/that nation. God determines the blessings, curses, or consequences these critics will see." (Remember Miriam and Aaron...and what happened when they just gossiped about Moses?)[16]

The application was pointed: Any church board being stingy with the pastor, and other workers, should not be surprised if God was stingy with them. They should try a generous approach and closely watch the results. Karen and I held our breath because both our church and we as pastors had been struggling financially. Yes, some important reasons led back to me. But our leadership now grasped that they were responsible for the church's penury, too.

They had wanted us to have adequate compensation, but the church *"...just did not have the money."* Reckoning without faith, this seemed to make sense. The church scraped along and Karen and I zipped our lips, watched the grocery list, and drove old cars.

After the seminar, the church board gave us a significant raise, and what happened was amazing: the income doubled the first month and the increases after that never stopped. This seminar was the financial foundation for our soon-to-come church building program. It continues. Recently the church gave $18,000 for Bibles in the Ukraine, and $51,000 to drill wells and construct churches in Africa.

It all works together, doesn't it? I had to show God I was serious about my commitment, and willing to just grow for God Himself "somewhere by Chicago". Then he released new ideas, new financial principles and new members. The church board blessed us. God blessed them.

After this, even Polson changed significantly. The city cleaned up the vacant lots, several streets were paved, and the Tribe got its college just a few miles down the road.

And yes, my wife and I purchased a lot in Lakeview Cemetery. It is sandwiched between the burial plot of Betty Ridenour, our church's very first convert in Polson (in 1945), and the grave of Corey Knipe. Betty was Bonnie Allred's older sister, and Corey was Bonnie's grandson. I had stood on that very ground twice and read about the resurrection. Next time someone else can do it ... for me. This burial hill was good enough for Dr. Teal and his wife from Chicago, and Betty Ridenour, and Corey Knipe. And it is good enough for us.

I will be buried in a casket with a good seal between the two lids because I detest the thought of cold water dripping on my stomach. And Karen's ashes will be in an urn a few feet above.

The Lord willing, of course.

Chapter 8
BLOSSOM, MARGE, TOMMY AND ME

In 1977 three people from the church and I found ourselves on a significant road trip. We had to stop at several restaurants, and we visited some tourist spots, like the Space Needle in Seattle. Whenever we walked into an establishment, everyone stopped talking and stared at us.

First came Blossom, then Tommy, followed by Marge, and finally me. It was Toad and Mole and Rat and Badger all over again, off on some wild adventure in the Willows. Or perhaps like the owl and the pussycat going to sea, in a beautiful pea-green boat.

"What are those people doing together? How in the world do they fit?"

They didn't have to say it: The question was on the minds of all who watched. It was like any healthy church when it's working right. One of the things I prayed for in my ministry was a good mix of people, a wide spectrum of different kinds. I hoped and prayed for young and old, intelligent and otherwise, wealthy and poor, good-looking and plain, skinny and fat, Republicans and Democrats.

I was in a discussion group at a conference once when a college student asked the visiting speaker,

"When your church has all one age or type of person in it, what do you have?"

And the speaker answered,

"You have a manipulated society."

Obviously our church was not manipulated. I tried that once and reefed on a lady in the hospital, there for a hysterectomy, to switch to our church from the Nazarenes. She had attended our denomination earlier in life, so I felt she was fair game. It worked. She switched, and talk about double trouble! I got into such a mess with that one, I told the Lord,

"Jesus, if you will just help me here, I promise I'll never do that again. I'm not going to ask for any more problems. I notice that in your life on earth, you didn't manipulate or discriminate. Nor did you have a Blackberry. You let the Holy Spirit schedule things, had your quiet time, got up and walked along some dusty path, and here they came. I'd like my ministry to be something like that. I don't want any problem people that I'm not supposed to have. If you bring someone, I'll try to minister to them, but I'm not going to ask for another Gayle. No way! Not ever!"

How dumb could I be anyway, dragging on someone who has just had a hysterectomy? Anyway, after that, right or wrong (which is debatable), I basically just let things happen, and watched to see who would come in the door.

One of the first was Blossom Cooper. After her death I heard a rumor that earlier in life, much earlier, she had been a fairly attractive woman of the night in our little town. If the rumor is true, by the time I arrived, Blossom had lost most of her petals and the old bloom was gone. Whatever her past, the years had been hard on her constitution. Maybe she was younger than she looked, but her appearance argued against that. Let me describe her as I knew her.

She had false teeth but wore them only when necessary, and at church it wasn't necessary. She also had a habit of sticking out her tongue, curled up in a "U". Her yellow-white hair was thin, which she tried to twist into a little bun. Much of the year she wore the same long, dark green coat and, to top off her *haute couture*, she wore tennis shoes. She lived in a tiny little shack down on what I called "poverty flats", the area behind then-named Rolfson's Building Supply, and her living room was dingy.

She had a wry sense of humor I could not pick up at times and a little bit of devilment in her. A lot of devilment. She would often call our home on a Monday and ask that I come over and pick up her "contribution". I would usually groan at the idea because it would only be a dollar or two, and then I was stuck for about an hour's worth of chit-chat. (As I said, I didn't know her rumored history in town, or I might not have gone at all: the pastor going, every Monday, to see a former prostitute?)[17] Furthermore, she'd always make me feel guilty about leaving when I did wrench myself away.

"Good grief, woman!" I'd think angrily to myself as I grumbled to my car, *"You were at church just yesterday! Why didn't you put it in the plate then, for crying out loud?"*

But the kicker came years later when someone told my wife that Blossom regularly said to people,

"You know, pastor only comes when he wants my money!"

Yes, Blossom was usually the first into the restaurant on this special trip. Her entrance alone would stop most conversations.

Then there was Tommy Sanford, about twenty years old. He was another of my first fifty attendees, starting not too long after I came. His story was tragic for he had been a star athlete in his high school days, but one day while riding a motorcycle on Rocky Point Road he was hit by a car. It damaged his mind some, though he could talk well and had a quick wit. He laughed easily.

After many operations and therapy he still had to labor at walking and you always feared he would trip on a threshold. Walking with a cane, he had to swing his right leg in a wide arc to get it in place. That leg was four inches shorter now, and came attached to a boot with a huge lift. It took him time to enter any restaurant, and Blossom waited inside between some tables while Marge and I followed slowly behind.

Marge...well, Marge is still, at ninety years of age, the queen of the church. Still beautiful, as she was then at age fifty, her laugh is infectious, and she is usually chuckling about something... pure merriment incarnate. She was our best resident evangelist and was always steering me to needy people, or inviting others to church...as she did "Bearshit Bill" Orton and his son, Bill Orton III. (Bearshit Bill got his nickname while at Montana State University. One day a bear wandered on campus and was frightened up a tree. Bill climbed up after the bear, yanked its tail, and scared the poop out of him. Guess who was in the line of fire!)

After Marge invited the Ortons to church that Saturday, the next evening at our service she got up and suggested we pray for a couple of sad and lonely men who might come that night. They needed to get saved. At that remark, Bearshit Bill and Bill III tapped her on the shoulder, smiled, and waved. They were already there. And already saved. Marge was always pulling that kind of thing.

Where were the four of us misfits going anyway? To a Kathryn Kuhlman meeting in Vancouver, BC.

Kuhlman was the main hope in the U.S. right then for any who looked (even wistfully) at healing evangelists, and Marge wanted Tommy healed. So she prayed and the Lord seemed to line up the trip money in unusual fashion. That's why the four of us jammed into my four-door Volkswagen Rabbit, the one where the trunk lock would sometimes stick and not open.

That happened on the trip. We went to bed one night at a motel, unable to retrieve our luggage, and so Marge washed her clothing before she went to bed. Her clothes were still wet in the morning, though, whereupon she wrapped herself in a bedspread and traipsed down the second-story outside hallway to my room, banged on my door and told me she had to have her clothes and her suitcase. (Anyone in earshot must have wondered why her clothes and her suitcase would be in *my* room.)

Thank God I got the trunk open.

As I also did when Blossom dirtied her pants at the Space Needle.

I prayed on the way to the car then, too, believe me!

On that occasion, Blossom was just too frightened to go up the Needle with us, so she stayed in the ground-level waiting room. We did point out the restroom to her, but she was so distracted and nervous she didn't hear. When we finally got back down, she jumped up, stamped her feet and swore loudly,

"Damn you guys! Staying up there so long! I shit my pants!"

While they were cleaning up in the restroom, Marge threw the soiled garments into the trash, but Blossom complained,

"*Don't do that! They're perfectly good. I'll just put them in this sack.*"

Marge left them in the trash.

Did Tommy get healed? I'm sorry to say, no he didn't. We watched as a lot of other people told of amazing things happening, and Wild Bill Bentz did have a very unusual incident happen at that meeting. But I haven't told you yet about Bill. He's another man that was in our church, our rollicking pea-green boat, but his is a story for another chapter. This one belongs to Blossom. And Tommy! And Marge! I was just along for the wonderful ride, as was true for all the succeeding years at New Life Christian Center in Polson, Montana.

Chapter 9
WILD BILL BENTZ

One day Bill Bentz burst into my office.

"Miles, stand up! Turn around!" he ordered as he barged through the door. I did what Bill requested, looking over my shoulder. He grabbed the seat of my pants with his right hand and lifted me off the floor. I weighed 170 pounds at the time so that wasn't easy, especially with that hand and arm. Just a short time before it had been hard for him to lift either of them six inches off an armrest.

"I tell you I'm HEALED!" said Bill with his voice loud and his eyes twinkling. And for the world it seemed to be true. I joined in the laughing and backslapping. It was a great moment.

Bill's story for me started one day when we were seated on a stool in Price's restaurant, joined by John Dutzar, the local Presbyterian pastor. I'd just heard that Bill had cancer of the lymph system, and so I quizzed him about his treatment. As we talked I mentioned a book, "God Can Do It Again" by Kathryn Kuhlman, which had stories of healing reportedly taking place while people just sat in various audiences. I didn't quite know what to make of it, but still I asked,

"Would you possibly want to read that book, Bill?"

"Sure!"

About a month later he gave it back and said,

"I read your book, and it was interesting, but it's not something for me. I've got great insurance, great doctors, and I'm a tough old goat, so I'll go ahead with surgery. Thanks, though, for your concern."

End of conversation. Or so I thought. About six months later, I received a telephone call from Bill to come to his house.

"Where is the next healing meeting of that woman?" were his first words. No small talk with this guy.

"I don't know, Bill. I don't keep up on that. Why?"

"Because I want to go, that's why. If you'll go with me, I'll go anywhere in the United States. I've just been told in Seattle by my Dr. that the cancer has flared again, and that's after a bunch of operations and a lot of money! I said to myself on the way home that if you would go with me, I would go to that lady's next meeting."

About five days later we pulled away from the curb in his nearly-new 1974 Chrysler Imperial. I was driving because Bill was in no shape for that. It was very questionable that we should be taking this trip at all because he was having extreme difficulty breathing and was coughing up large quantities of mucous. He was weak and barely able to talk.

"I still want to go. Let's GO!" he ordered over my protestations. *"We'll stop in Missoula and get this junk cleaned out!"*

At St. Patrick's Hospital in Missoula, we discovered that someone in our local hospital had fitted Bill with a tracheotomy breathing-tube sized for a baby, not the largest size a big man needed. After that was discovered and after they vacuumed out his nearly-full lungs, Bill was breathing deeply, smiling broadly, and we hit the freeway. This was Friday. The meeting was Sunday afternoon in Los Angeles.

Our first stop was Salmon, Idaho, where we had a bowl of soup before we turned in for the night. Bill couldn't swallow a spoonful. In fact, he'd cough, and the soup would shoot out his new tracheotomy tube. Suddenly I wasn't as hungry as I'd thought.

His cancer had started in the lymph nodes under his right arm, in the right shoulder and was now invading his neck, hence the difficulty breathing and eating. I noticed, too, that over the whole trip west, Bill would at times groan quietly, rubbing his right shoulder, and he couldn't lift his arm much at all. But that didn't keep him from talking, even if his voice was guttural and raspy and he had to place his finger over the tracheotomy to speak. The car became Bill's confessional booth. He talked almost nonstop through Idaho and Nevada.

It was apparent why his name became "Wild Bill" to those who knew him. The stories were not pretty. They covered his childhood, teens, his time as a sailor, and up to the present. He obviously needed to breathe out the foul details. His revelations astounded me.

Protestants have been the losers for eliminating this source of healing for sinners, as have their converts. It's one thing to confess aloud with the congregation each Sunday that you have sinned in doing things you shouldn't, and not doing things you should, but it's a whole different assignment to do a "moral inventory" with someone such as Alcoholics Anonymous requires.

"Confess your faults to one another that you might be healed!" says the Bible.[18] Under our Protestant bandaids and scabs, under our repressions and denials, our lying and silence, there are pockets of moral pus that need to drain. I've heard all my life that sinners

only need to confess to God, and not to some religious "Father", but our protests are often slick avoidance of a healing kind of pain. It is only as we bring the horror of our failures into the light of some serious confession that we can be led into deep sorrow for our sinning, begin the true work of repentance, and see even more clearly why we need a Savior.

The Long Beach Municipal Auditorium was full hours before the service began at 2:00 PM Sunday afternoon. I knew it would be, so I pressed to get us there early, and we did make it onto the main floor but just barely. We were seated against the back wall under the first balcony. Finally the action began, which means that Kathryn Kuhlman finally appeared and said,

"Helllllooooo, Beloved!!!! Have you been...waiting...for me?" The word *"waiting"* was dragged out unnervingly, and the words, *"... for me"* were oddly staccato and cryptic. But the place roared.

Then came the long sermon, and Bill became impatient:

"When's the line going to start?"

"Bill, I've told you, there won't be any line. If you're healed, you're healed in your seat!"

"OH!" he said dejectedly, and it wasn't two minutes and he was asleep. Now I was bummed, too. I was hoping this whole venture would at least get this guy "saved" if not healed. And here he was, missing a good sermon on conversion.

Suddenly, though, things shifted. Kuhlman started calling people out of the audience, those she sensed were healed of this or that. For a couple of hours there was a steady stream of people onto the platform, telling their stories, crying and laughing, and even falling over backwards *"under the power"*, a very odd curiosity of these meetings. There were appointed "catchers" watching for people to fall backwards like a tree. (Try it. Can you do it without trying to catch yourself?) Even then they would not catch the fall of some fashionable woman and her head would bounce on the hardwood of the stage with a solid *thunk* you could hear in the third balcony. It was enough to keep even Bill awake.

It finally wound down to a final sermonette, again about the need for salvation, about becoming a Christian, and Bill fell asleep again. The moment the altar call was given, however, a river of people started streaming down the aisle, and my charge woke up with a start:

"What's happening? What's going on?"

"Well, she just asked if there were anyone here who hadn't given themselves to Christ, to come up front and do it."

"Have I done that?"

"If you don't know, then you probably haven't!"

"Well, should I?"

"Sure!"

Bill was in the aisle immediately.

I finally caught up with him halfway to the stage, the point where the stream of humanity stopped. With the aisles plugged, Kuhlman asked them to pray a prayer of commitment with her. Everyone (except Bill and me) bowed their heads. He just stared at Miss Kuhlman and I stared at him. I saw no words forming on his lips. But I did notice an important detail: at her request for everyone to put up a hand in prayer, Bill obeyed and put his right arm up as straight as a fencepost (the one he had been rubbing constantly, could hardly lift, and was groaning about the whole trip). It stayed there for the entire long prayer. As soon as Miss Kuhlman said *"Amen!"* Bill asked too loudly,

"What happens now?"

"People head for their cars," I whispered.

"Let's get out of here!" he ordered in his loud tracheotomy voice. So with him plowing a wake through the people behind us, we two were some of the first to make it to our car.

"Well, nothing happened here. Guess we go to Sacramento!"

Miss Kuhlman had another meeting on Tuesday night there. Over the next two days, Bill kept trying to eat, but he couldn't swallow a full bite. It was miserable watching him, and frightening. When the meeting came Tuesday night, we weren't as fortunate in our placement, for we found ourselves in the third balcony this time, and the stage was a mile away, but something happened anyway. Bill did seem to be distinctly singled out by Kuhlman through her claimed gift of discernment or special knowledge.

"Up there in the third balcony," she said, *"God is touching someone. It's a man."*

That's all she said, and then shifted her attention to other people on the main floor. But a few minutes later, she again pointed at the third balcony.

"I have to go back to the third balcony. A little bit to my left."

She was pointing directly at us now:

"Sir, you have not been able to swallow. You can now. You try it. You will now be able to swallow."

I looked at Bill, he looked at me, and he left immediately saying,

"I need a drink of water!"

And it was true. Bill was able to swallow. My, but could he ever! That very night we went to a Chinese restaurant, and he chowed down a huge amount. The next day when we arrived in Jackpot, Nevada, on the way home, the first thing he did was hit a blackjack table, made a quick $45, and we headed for the dining room. There Bill topped off a huge meal with *five* (I counted them) pieces of pie! I will never forget his raspy, crackling voice as he excitedly called his wife,

"Jewell, you won't believe how much I ate! Ha! Ha! Ha! Ha!"

I wished she had seen it.

It was shortly after that he burst into my office and hoisted me off the floor. He was so convinced he was healed that he bought a new pickup, a new car and thirty new furnaces for his shop's inventory. Now from gratitude he promised to put a new copper spire on the church.

Kathryn Kuhlman had not said he was *healed,* though. That became apparent, of course. But he kept attending Miss Kuhlman's meetings: four more in fact. Something unusual happened at every single meeting. In Vancouver, BC, for instance, the one Blossom, Marge, Tommy and I had attended, Bill had rudely elbowed his way to the head of a long outside line.

Just inside the main doors, one of the last people admitted, he suddenly threw up his last meal and plugged his tracheotomy tube. He dropped to his knees on the floor where he could well have died from choking, but an alert usher had been watching, one who had some previous experience with a tracheotomy and he knew exactly what to do. He took out his pocket knife, cut the cord holding the inner of the two tubes, and pulled the appliance out of Bill's neck. Crisis solved. Something of similar magnitude happened at every meeting Bill attended.

Through all this travel and action, the cancer kept eating through the skin of his neck, and spread from ear to ear under his chin. It was ghastly, looking like chicken guts. As he got worse, I baptized him by sprinkling at the hospital, and kept close vigil with his lovely wife, Jewell, and his son, Ed. But he died at age fifty-two, not by choking to death on his own blood as was expected but quietly, peacefully. His heart just stopped. I was amazed at that. Bill was still a strong man.

Before he died, however, we had a wonderful day at his home. I think I'll tell you about that next when I share the story of Barney Johnson, his hired hand. It fits best there.

Chapter 10
THE BAPTISM OF
BARNEY JOHNSON

"Barney! Go after Barney!" said Bill that memorable day in his home. The command was given in its usual guttural way as Bill covered the hole of his tracheotomy with the index finger.

We were just sitting there at that moment, both of us savoring a highly important time of shared insight. Bill had been hard to communicate with, and he hadn't previously been open to much theological or spiritual input. Totally in command of his life, the spiritual had never been important, so it really was hard for him to shift toward spiritual things.

He had been a man of action and physical accomplishment. Money and sheet metal and furnaces and business...and for years alcohol...had been his world. Of course his family got short-sheeted. I was discouraged at his spiritual disinterest because Bill was on his way out. We both knew a few short weeks would finish his story. Up to this day all he had mostly been interested in getting healed of his cancer.

I gave it another stab, took communion over to him that day, and he was actually listening for once. He asked the significance of this act. Where did it come from? Why do we do this odd thing anyway?

In my explanation, I took it back to Moses and the children of Israel and how, on that first Passover, the people of God were instructed to take a lamb, kill it, drain the blood into a basin, and then spread it over the doorposts of their home. That blood would show the angel of death, coming that night, which home was Egyptian and which was Hebrew. When he saw blood on a doorpost, the angel would "pass over" that house and head on down the block. Then I explained to Bill that Jesus was the Lamb of God, and the shedding of His blood for us was much more significant than the blood of the little lambs killed before the Hebrew exodus.

"Bill, when you allow Christ to be your Savior by making Him your Lord, then by that simple act what you do is paint His blood over your own spiritual door, the eternal part of yourself, and you are by that act of faith (and obedience) spared from a more important death, a second death, a spiritual death that happens to people who reject God. We can die twice, Bill. You will die physically, perhaps quite soon. But after that, there is a far worse death, when you are forever separated from God. People who have always told God to 'get lost' are going to get their wish, if they reject Him long enough. But if you have the blood of Christ above your spiritual door when you die physically, you are 'passed over' at that second death, and you live forever."

Bill got it that time, and I could hardly believe we finally connected. He understood the huge significance of Jesus' death and the blood of Christ, the partial "why" of the Eucharist. We prayed together like we never had before. We had Communion, as we call the Eucharist, and I've never celebrated one more moving or joyful. As we sat there quietly afterward, Bill said an incredible thing:

"You know, Miles, I thank God today for my cancer, even if I die with it. I never would have understood what you just said, I never would have been ready for eternity, if I had not had cancer."

I replied,

"Bill, if you went through all of life without any problem, without any suffering or reversals, without any jail time or pain, and you woke up one day in hell because of a lifetime of sunny weather, I can imagine you in hell, shaking your fist at God Himself, saying, 'Why didn't you give me cancer? Why didn't I go through divorce or bankruptcy? Why didn't you send me to prison? I might have awakened then from my happy and self-contented stupor, my self-sufficiency, and listened to those who told me about Christ!'"

I tell you, I was happy in a sad way by Bill's grave when recalling this day, and I was pleased again when talking later to his son.

"Ed, how would your dad have handled his cancer if he had not connected with Christ?"

"He would have shot himself!"

But now let's switch to Barney Johnson who was Bill's main hired man.

He was a shy man and he also had some trouble with drink, so he never made it too high on the town's social register. He lived in a small home by the Ranch Restaurant, a popular local eating spot. Faithful and dependable at work, he must have done much of the actual sheet metal fabrication. Bill would sell the furnaces and get the orders for the consequent sheet-metal parts, but Barney would use those amazing tools to bend the tin into shapes I couldn't imagine or believe. I went into that dingy little place, littered with sharp tin clippings, several times before I ever really got acquainted with either Bill or Barney. I always marveled at how those complicated shapes came out of a flat sheet of tin.

So I did *"go after"* Barney after Bill died. Barney himself got cancer and his daughter and son-in-law attended our church, so at their urging and with Bill's command in mind, I went over and shared Christ with him. I can't say that I personally "got him" because Christ is the One who did that, but Barney did pray aloud his commitment to Christ that day, and I was hoping that Bill was somehow able to watch and hear that moment, one laden with the weight of glory.

By now we were finally in the new church, but just barely. No more borrowing the baptistry at the Christian Church (where I once forgot I was filling it and flooded part of their sanctuary). We could now do it in our own building where the fiberglass baptismal tank was installed in the dining room. It was handy to both the main bathrooms, where the candidates would dress before and after the ceremony.

Barney had a wooden leg and he didn't want to baptize that, so we put him in the ladies' room for preparation because it was closest to the action. He had two grown sons, both of them caught up in the hippy revolution happening right then. Barney chose them for his attendants as he approached the baptismal waters, and they both seemed honored to help.

The dining room was full to capacity because this was our first baptism in the new church, and because it was Barney. We all waited expectantly for the trio to appear and finally the door opened: here they came...Barney and his boys, his arms draped around their necks. With their long hair and hippy clothes, and with Barney's empty pantleg, they made quite a sight as they thumped toward the tub.

But about half-way there it happened. *Barney's pants fell down*, exposing his boxer shorts for the whole crowd to see. The room fell absolutely silent, all of us staring at the crumpled pants, the yellowed shorts and one bony leg. Barney looked helplessly down, quickly realized his predicament, and suddenly said,

"Oh, GOD! Pull 'em UP!"

Amazingly, not a single person snickered. There were children and teens present, of course, and over 200 others. But no one made a sound. The pants were pulled up by one of his boys, we somehow got Barney into the tank, and the wonderful deed was eventually done. It was only after we had sung, *"I have decided to follow Jesus; no turning back!"* and after I had given the benediction, that the place erupted. The chuckles and laughter had been held long enough, for the incident was indeed hilarious. But by then Barney didn't mind and chuckled himself.

I talked with him about it later at his home. He said,

"You know, I almost didn't wear my shorts!"

Chapter 11
THIS IS THE STRANGEST THING

Bonnie Allred asked the question out of the blue. She and Bertie Coverdell were in the church kitchen having lunch, the only two people who had shown up that day for the Women's Missionary Council.

"Would the church be interested in the Guineer property?"

I thought to myself: *"Yeah. We need to be buying property! Hardly any money in savings. Two women at WMC's working on a quilt. Fat chance."*

"I don't know. Where is it?" I replied.

I might as well follow the rabbit trail for a little while. Bonnie gave the location, and told how the large family wanted to sell the farm since both the parents had died. I was interested in the fact that, whatever it was, it was located quite near the new $12 million high school being built right then.

After sharing a bite of their lunch, I got on my bicycle and pedaled up the hill. Coming to the end of the last paved street, I bumped up one of the two tire tracks into the old farmhouse yard, and started to chuckle at the school board for their mistake: they were building the huge new school without having obtained any deeded access. They were land-locked! I was still shaking my head in disbelief when I stopped, turned around, and looked back over the town. Suddenly there was a *whoosh* through my spirit, followed by a very strong one-word thought:

"*YES!*"

Instantly I saw the desirability of the location: on the north side, there was a commanding view over the town and Flathead Lake sweeping up toward Canada; on the east the Missions jutted up in Rocky Mountain grandeur; on the west was a wonderful fourteen-acre parcel available for an entire campus and not just a church; and on the south was the soon-to-be-very-busy high school.

What about a road to our church and the school both? It was obvious. It would happen. It would be constructed according to tough specifications *right along this particular property,* at taxpayers' expense.

I thought it a wonderful idea, but to my conservative mind the thought of our acquiring it was preposterous. Since we had a board business meeting coming up in a few days though, I did put it on the agenda, but sixth-place in importance. The board would see it but demurely not notice, and it would quietly slip out of future consideration or they would reject the idea out of hand.

But I was wrong. Keith Armstrong, still on the governing board, took a quick look at the agenda and said,

"*I think we ought to seriously consider this sixth item first. In fact I think we should look at it and vote tonight to actively pursue this* *property. I can think of a way we could come up with the $26,000 the owners want. We would borrow money from ourselves at 7% and give ourselves 20-year notes."*

So the board piled in cars and we drove to the property. It was four acres, half of it a flat bench, the rest a slope that would easily work with a daylight basement. There was a perfect place for a parking lot right by the street, an irrigation canal between it and the school property adjoining it, and it had two old houses on it: the first "stick" home ever built in Polson, and a smaller house built for hired hands. The vote was unanimous: we needed to get on this and pray for God's blessing.

Some of the selling family didn't want a church there. Others were glad they had an offer and could settle the estate. Their final vote gave us the property. In addition, we immediately had the $26,000 needed to complete the deal, borrowing from ourselves.

Our present building, full twice each Sunday, was becoming a fire trap for all jammed in there with its single chute of an entrance/exit. Our Sunday school classes were farmed out to awkward locations, as were our many mid-week Bible study groups. We needed to act.

So the board authorized my taking an exploratory trip to visit Idaho, Washington, Oregon and California, to investigate congregations building a new facility, or those who had good over-all ideas. I examined at least twenty different situations, compiling ideas, asking questions, noticing what cost too much, and what was doable for us.

One church in Medical Lake, Washington, caught our eye. They had built it for eight dollars per square foot, an unbelievable price (because the pastor had done much of the work). The board traveled there on a junket, and we got a copy of their plans. Back home we laid them out and studied them in relation to our building lot. Sadly, the plan didn't seem to fit...until...Dr. Terry Lanes said,

"Why don't we make the floor plan fit our site? Why not stretch it out along the hill, modify it, throw in an angle for variety and distinction, but include the same basic components?"

His comment struck such fire with me that I went home that very night and drew up a rough plan incorporating his suggestion.

For a feasibility study, the board decided to approach the engineer and architect for the Outlaw Inn in nearby Kalispell. Just finished at that time, it was the area's latest success. The two men agreed to study our plan and whether we could consider building it for around $275,000.

The architect finally got back to us *four months later*, December 17, 1976. We wanted to start building the spring of 1977!

"There's no way you can build this!" was his first remark as he threw down our plan. *"Not on your budget! Here is what you can do for your money!"*

He then spread out the plans for some First Baptist Church, a woefully-inadequate suggestion with folding doors everywhere and only two offices. We were plunged into sticker-shock. This was all that was feasible? We ended the meeting in discouragement and confusion.

I had a picture in mind of a building that would fit our floor plan, however, and over that holiday period I constructed a mat-board model of what I envisioned. While a young boy, I had constructed some model buildings out of balsawood for my train set, and during high school I had taken mechanical drawing, but otherwise I had no training whatever in architecture. God gave me the ability, though, to visualize objects in my mind and also the ability to draw my little model to scale. January 5, 1977, the nine men wandered into the boardroom and were stunned. They took a serious thirty-minute look at the model, and said,

"That's IT!"

All I can say is that God either gave us a gift of ignorance or a gift of faith. We disagreed with the architect that we couldn't do what we thought. We paid him for his feasibility study and dismissed him. We decided that I would confer with the engineer, Thor Jackola, through the planning process, and that his draftsman would draw up our plans.

That decision was stunning to me. The board was approving $17,000 for *pieces of paper?* When we had such a dismal financial history? Committing to a building costing at least $275,000, and we didn't have a cent of it?

Suddenly I was traveling back and forth to Kalispell to discuss the plans, for our little model was not only good for the board's visioning, but also for the engineer's and the draftsman's. It wasn't two months and the building's plans were drawn. Originally, we were only serious about finishing the main floor, but on one of my trips the draftsman said,

"It would only take a few hours to draw up a suggested floorplan for the basement level, so could you possibly give me some idea of where you're going?"

In just *ten minutes* I sliced up the entire 10,000 sq. feet of basement space, and today it is almost exactly like the building stood in 2003 when I retired. By way of comparison, I spent five years thinking through the insignificant details of my retirement home finished in 2004. Obviously, God was with us, and He wanted that building built. For some fun reason, I was a part of the process.

Rev. Linfield Crowder, one of our denomination's evangelists, told us during a crusade that we really should be thinking of building, and also gave a powerful epigram:

"Action draws action, and people draw people!"

What a God-given word for us! Our action did draw action. When those plans were done, they were already paid for! And the land was also paid for! The unusualness of this encouraged us to keep going. Unbelievably, we were ready to start digging on a 22,700 square foot building, five times the size of our old facility.

On June 21, 1977, we started pouring $35,000 worth of concrete, not having the money, but it was there when the cement work was done. Next we ordered the $41,000 worth of laminated beams, not having the money, but the money was there when they arrived. On September 21, we started framing with an eleven-man crew, not having the money, but it came in while we were building.

The laminated beams, needed all over the site, did not come for five months after the order. So we built every component together we possibly could as we waited, keeping all our crew busy. One Friday night, however, we could advance not one board more without those beams.

The next morning the truck pulled onto the lot!

Our engineer had done a marvelous job of designing pre-cut and pre-formed components for the floor system and trusses for both ends of the building, so the building shot up like a mushroom. When the beams were in place, the remaining structure was soon framed and sheathed, and on November 15, 1977, (under two months from the start of the framing), we had on the roof plywood and all but thirty squares of shingles in place. It was a Wednesday night. We just might beat the weather after all.

No such luck. That very night a six-inch snowstorm struck, and it was predicted we were heading into a bad winter. One of Montana's chinook winds came roaring through on Thursday night and Friday, however, so on Saturday we pulled together the only fully volunteer crew we ever had and were able to slap on twenty squares of shingles in one day.

The following Monday, Nov. 21, we were able to set the regular crew on the remaining ten squares and fully weatherproof the roof. Two days later another big snowstorm arrived and the snow, that winter, never melted off.

An electrician, just bankrupted, gave us a marvelous price for stringing seven miles of conduit and wire. While he and his helpers were wiring the building, the temperature was seventeen degrees below zero for a solid month.

A semi-truck of 5/8-inch sheetrock, 95,000 square feet of it, was stranded in Missoula and we got it all for a very good price. That was exactly the amount needed for the building. But there was one incident that for me stood out above all others, showing the goodness and grace of God, and the unusual nature of this project.

One day Jim Whartman, an artistic church member working for us, was available to construct our sanctuary lighting fixtures. We had figured out a nice design using rough wood, ordinary plumbing and electrical parts, and even sections of irrigation pipe. But we had not ordered any hardware for those lights. Suddenly, Jim could work on them.

As I went downtown to see what was available, the store "Coast-to-Coast" popped into my mind. Oddly, I first went every other possible place to check on those hundreds of little items. No one had any of them in that quantity. Finally I followed the original hunch, went to Coast-To-Coast and started asking,

"Do you have 120 of this type of item?"

"Yes, I think I do!"

"And how about 120 nipples like this?"

"Yup!"

"How about seventy-five feet of chain this size?"

"I've had some chain that dimension on a roll for two years."

When we unrolled it, it was seventy-five feet long. On and on, through item after item we went, until we had everything assembled. As he was adding up the items, the owner stopped adding, looked at the unusual collection, and said,

"This is the strangest thing: Except for the chain, everything you picked up today came in by mistake."

Financially, we borrowed $120,000 from ourselves, giving on-demand notes at 7% interest. We borrowed another $120,000 from the bank on a twenty-year repay. In order to get the bank money, eleven of us, including myself, had to sign a note for the entire $120,000 (each of us) so that if a default took place, they could go after each one of us in turn to be sure to get their money. Me? Sign for $120,000? On my salary? With my assets? Insane! But it was just as bad for most of the others. (By the way, I am not recommending this. We even found out later that government regulations would not have allowed this approach to our financing.)

Not everyone was impressed. One popular builder in the area at that time said to me,

"You will NEVER fill that hole."

A strong Christian and respected businessman in the congregation came to me about this policy of borrowing:

"Pastor, we are making a huge mistake here, borrowing this money! David Wilkerson has just written a book, THE VISION, and in it he counsels all Christians and churches not to go into debt."

But the board still felt God was in this whole project, David Wilkerson's advice notwithstanding, so we rifled the general fund every single month of the two-year building program and received no large bequests whatever. Ours was not a wealthy congregation. We accomplished what we did with only 60% of 120 members and 20% of the "adherents" actually tithing (according to our treasurer). God still met all our needs. We even bumped our giving to "missions" from 2% of the general fund up to 10%, during the building project, because we felt it was wrong for the people to be asked to tithe if our corporation were not doing it also. We decided that 10% of the general fund had to go to causes not benefiting our local congregation in any way.

And how much did the finished building end up costing? $475,000. We made up the extra $200,000 above our initial projection out of the general fund, and met every "on-demand" in-church promissory note at the moment it was submitted. If the note from the congregation was $500, the money was there. If it was $5000, the same. Once our savings built up to $22,000, and I watched carefully. Sure enough, the man who had loaned us $22,000 wanted his money. It was there. Only one time was the money not there, a moment in our church when an unwise payroll raise was given, a decision about which I was very uneasy. That time, in six moths, we fell behind by half the very amount voted for pay raises. It was the only time, with all of our "on-demand" notes that we had to borrow to redeem one.

One more financial detail: in the first seven years of my ministry in Polson, we were only able to pay $7000 on the indebtedness I inherited as pastor. In the seven years from 1975 to 1982 while we were building, the congregation was able to meet $700,000 worth of budget items.

Yes, Jim (at Coast-to-Coast), it was the strangest thing how that building came together. Not just the parts for the light fixtures. Everything.

Chapter 12
KEITH AND DOLLY ARMSTRONG

He stood there that day with the key in his hand, fearing he was the only man and his the only family coming to church again. Should he unlock the door, or should he just call it quits and admit his dream for a church in Polson was a mistake? He was the only financial supporter, there was no pastor at the moment, and his family didn't like the long drive because they didn't even live in Polson but in St. Ignatius, twenty-eight miles to the South.

"Why am I doing this anyway?"

Keith had been born in Pablo, a tiny town five miles south of Polson. His mother was an admirable Christian and strong individual. She reared Keith and two other children by herself, passing along a strong faith and commitment, certainly to Keith. Somehow in the development of his faith he got a vision for a church in Polson.

After high school Keith joined the Marines. Assigned to the South Pacific, he was there during much of the WWII conflict and narrowly escaped death on numerous occasions. His close encounters started early, the day two large ships departed from Hawaii for the Pacific war theater. That day the soldiers and marines were lined up in row, made to count off by twos, the "ones" directed to one battleship, the "twos" to another. He was a number "two", and didn't think much about it until he heard later that the other battleship was torpedoed a day out of harbor and every man aboard was lost. They never found the wreckage. The man on each side of Keith had counted the wrong number: he was the one of the three that lived.

Another close shave happened when a kamikaze pilot targeted his ship near Iwo Jima. Keith was an excellent marksman and good with all guns, partly because of his love for hunting. That day when the ship alarm sounded they were in the sights of a suicide bomber coming in on his side of the ship. He rushed to his .50 caliber machine gun and started to fill the air with the hot bullets and tracers while the plane flew directly at him, also continuously firing his machine guns, not just at the ship, but directly at Keith. The fighter's bullets raked the deck on both sides of his turret, peeling off the heavy wood and rolling it up like a rug. But Keith, with steady hand and steely eye, kept firing and he won the duel. The fireball of death exploded short of its target and fell harmlessly into the sea right by the ship.

After the war and after college, Keith was hired by the National Forest Service and was assigned to a unit near Libby, Montana. Traveling home during that time in a work pickup, he did not know the muffler system was leaking, and again he almost died, this time from carbon-monoxide poisoning. The effects of that stayed with him the rest of his life. It frequently made him agitated and he would sigh aloud, even during worship.

Shortly after Keith wondered if he should open the church or just quit, the church hired John Weaver for its pastor. Keith was the only man on the board, the only one paying the pastor's salary and most of the congregational expenses. He mustered the $35/week salary (1956) and John worked at other jobs as the two men crippled along trying to gain momentum. The Catholics, Methodists, and Presbyterians all had well-established congregations and few people in the community were welcoming to this newcomer-church. They looked with skepticism and various degrees of opposition at this Pentecostal upstart.

So times were still hard at Polson Assembly of God not only for Keith, but for Pastor Weaver as well. His family was growing, he had to work at odd jobs to survive, and Keith felt more and more guilty for submitting John to starvation wages. One night Keith and Dolly asked John and Teenie for dinner, and after the meal Keith motioned for John to join him in the living room.

"Pastor, Dolly and I have decided that it is just plain wrong for the church to be paying you such a poor wage, so we have decided to mortgage our house to change that."

John was deeply moved by the generosity and thoughtfulness of this offer, but he replied,

"Keith, let's not do that yet. Instead let's just really pray that God will bring new people with that added income. Let's try that and see what happens."

Almost immediately both prayers were answered. The church was now on better financial footing with the addition of new people. When John left the church for Bozeman he was receiving $85/week, and there were twenty-nine members on the roll plus a good number of other "adherents".

At this point: TA DA! Enter Miles Finch.

Oh, my! Poor Keith! Here came decline and pressure, another young pastor to adjust to, and the renewed assignment to keep this church financially afloat. Keith kept his balance, however, and his marvelous spirit, and God pulled him through.

He stood supportively by me, even though I lied to him and to the rest of the board one very important evening. I was supposed to have taken care of some detail, but Keith was careful about things, and he knew (he had checked) that I had not done what I promised to do. During the meeting he asked me if I had attended to the matter, and yes, I had. Keith thus caught me in a bald-faced lie, and immediately blew the whistle. With all of them darkly looking at me I knew there was only one thing to do: confess my sin, sincerely ask their forgiveness, and request another chance.

They graciously did so, but Keith had a lot to do with it. As board chairman and the most trusted man of the church, his opinion was the majority opinion. It was because of his goodness and grace that I still had a church and a job. Although I'm sure he watched me carefully for a good period, he never brought it up again. He never mentioned the incident to his wife.

Over the years Keith was always ready to accept new assignments of faith. Right after he retired, he became the church's main supervisor for our building project. It was his idea to borrow from ourselves at 7%, and his was the largest amount loaned on the hairy-scary financial plan that carried the day. He signed, with ten others of us, for the $120,000 loan at the bank (responsible for the whole amount if none of the others came through); he found the main framing crew that coordinated things so well; he was on the job every day, faithfully checking all details; and he allowed me to make important architectural decisions even when he strongly disagreed a time or two. He stayed with the project until its completion and gave me his personal set of plans when the job was done.

After Keith had served thirty-five years as the main man on our church board we started the systematic rotation of all board members. It must have been hard for Keith to relinquish his position of privilege and importance, but he did it with gracious acceptance. How rare is that?

An opportunity then came for him to join a church-building project in his own hometown of St. Ignatius. Since his vision for Polson was now fact, he felt it only logical that he lend his aid to a church in his own locality. Again he became the main person on the project and again the Kingdom of God gained a beautiful new church, complete with parsonage.

It was not too long afterwards that Keith discovered he had terminal cancer. One day when we were sharing old times and memories I asked him,

"Keith, from your perspective right now, what would you advise me as a younger man?" Instantly he replied,

"I'd quit sooner."

When it came time to retire, I remembered that, and for one last grateful time, I took his advice.

And Dolly? What kind of woman would be willing to drive twenty-eight miles, often more than once a week, to help her husband pioneer a church? Who would help keep two children willing to travel to a place where there were no other youth? How could she agree to mortgage her rather small home for the pastor's salary, or be happy over the years with wood heat and little remodeling so that Keith could continue pursuing his dream?

This lady was remarkable as well because she was always bright and cheerful with a marvelous laugh and sense of humor. She would often just shake her head, roll her eyes and exclaim,

"Oh, that's Keith!"

One day after Keith died and she had moved to Polson, Dolly asked Karen to take her to Super One. She wasn't feeling the best that day, but still wanted to get groceries anyway. As they entered the store, Dolly turned green. Karen grabbed a red bowl on sale, and got it under Dolly's chin just in time.

Home they went. Going back to the store later, Karen took the bowl from the parking lot into the restroom to clean and then went to the checkstand where she told the clerk what happened.

"Oh, everyone in the store knows about it already," said the smiling woman.

Dolly was always our church's poet laureate, and many occasions found her composing a sonnet or a contrapuntal commemoration of the event. That's what she did this time, too.

Keith and Dolly Armstrong: *wonderful* people! Crucial to the existence of our church! That's why the church's dining area is named "The Armstrong Room". Everyone entering the church sees their name immediately.

Chapter 13
SURPRISED BY PRIDE

LEADERSHIP JOURNAL, a Christianity Today, Inc. publication, printed this chapter, with additional material, on pp. 45–49 of its Spring 2007 issue.

I was sitting on the platform with my eyes sweeping the congregation just before worship began. Why, *there* was a family from the Methodist church! And over *there* was one from the Presbyterians! The crowd was really good-sized this Sunday... more people in the balcony than I'd seen.

"Oh, praise You, Lord! Thank you, Jesus! This is wonderful!"

I have always loved sitting in the chancel, observing. It offers a perspective from which to refresh my memory of what God has been doing. Over there and back there were the two couples whose marriages are solid and intact even though an emotional affair (between them) had been involved. Up there was the couple, she a hippie and Buddhist, he from an Italian Catholic background who connected with Christ in our fellowship and were leading our thriving youth group.

Back under the balcony was a beautiful young woman who had come to Christ and was changed from a wild twenty-something to a girl with a shining face. Every Christian sitting in our church that day was a chronicle of grace. Every face represented an interesting and colorful spiritual history and here I was, getting to sit on the front row observing these lives!

I recalled the group of professional men from our little main street with whom I met for coffee. Harry made the group difficult at times. Whenever I saw him in the group, I was tempted to forget coffee that day. Involved in a church music program, he often seemed a cynical agnostic if not atheist. He could be pleasant and could add interesting items to the conversation, but he could also uncork occasionally. Right after a Good Friday service, for instance, I was standing by the host pastor when Harry blasted him:

"Who allowed them to sing that shit?"

One morning at coffee he was ranting about churches being leeches on society. The moment grew in awkwardness because most of the guys were from different churches around town. Finally I wished aloud that he could just join me one Sunday on my perch in the church, and let me point out some wonderful stories sitting in the pews. What would have happened to the children of those two couples who had just about divorced? Why was it possible for the two couples to remain in our church and still be friends after that sticky entanglement? What trail of devastation and woe would have followed them and their children if Christ had not intervened?

And what about that young woman back under the balcony who had been spared by Christ from a life of prostitution, abortions, and who knows what else? What amount of money had the government saved in various welfare or incarceration costs, various remedial programs and emergency room charges?

I concluded my rebuttal:

"Why, the savings to society and government would be huge, from our church alone. Couple ours with all the other churches in town, and the term 'leech' doesn't fit, does it Harry?"

He sat silent. It was a satisfying moment, one that seemed to justify all of this coffee time I'd been having.

But the Sunday to which I referred above was different for me somehow. I was enjoying this, feeling the "anointing", when out of the blue came a thought very contrary to all of this pleasure:

"Miles, Miles, MILES! Take a look at yourself. A long, hard look. Is what you are feeling my 'anointing', or is it possibly...pride? Are you so thrilled by your success and the church's progress right now that you are putting a good twist on some very dark things in yourself?"

It was not only possible. I had to admit it was the truth. Yes, there was a dark stain spreading over my heart, the darkest sin of all, the sin by which the devil became the devil.

"Pride," writes C.S. Lewis, *"gets no joy out of having something, only out of having more of it than the next man. We say that people are proud of being rich, or clever, or good-looking, but they are not. They are proud of being richer, or cleverer, or better-looking than others.... It is the comparison that makes you proud, the pleasure of being above the rest. Once the element of competition has gone, pride has gone."* [19]

And I was right there. We were currently The Church of the Holy Anointing! We had more momentum, more of the Spirit of God on us, better music, and a nicer building than anyone but the Catholics (and maybe even a better one than theirs, for practical purposes anyway, and for less money).

We preached the Word of God better. We were more right on baptism, on giving, on evangelism, on just about everything.

It was clear that we had a relationship with Jesus that was just a little closer than was true of the other churches in town.

None of these things were said aloud, of course, none of them were squarely faced, but this was the attitude developing.

"The real black, diabolical pride comes when you look down on others so much that you do not care what they think of you. Of course, it is very right, and often our duty, not to care what people think of us, if we do so for the right reason; namely, because we care so incomparably more what God thinks. But the proud man has a different reason for not caring. He says, 'Why should I care for the applause of that rabble as if their opinion were worthy anything?'" [20]

I've always loved C.S. Lewis' writings, and had referred to his chapter called "The Great Sin" in *Mere Christianity* many times. Now the sledgehammer of this truth fell directly on me.

I was almost nauseous that morning from the insight, and for weeks I reflected on and reevaluated everything I was doing, everything our church was doing.

I saw how widespread this temptation is. One group thinks it has more apostolic seniority and authority than others. Another is more intellectual, or more orderly and decent, or more inclusive. Still others see themselves better evangelists than everyone else, the only ones hitting the streets.

More than! Better than! Every group has its point of pride.

It's easy and certainly right for church leaders...all Christians really...to desire more of God and His gifts. That can be good. Aspiring to be closer to Him, and to be more effective in His Kingdom is a given of the Christian life. Of course God wants aspiration. He also wants us to be as effective as we can for His Kingdom. And for some that can mean amazing results.

But aspiration is different from ambition.

The ambition I fear springs from the rancid soil of pride, the secret desire within an individual or group to tap the power of God and the dynamic of the Holy Spirit for purposes of preeminence. Our imaginations flash at the thought of all the attention, the adulation, the attainment. Why, we could have the largest, most wealthy and generous church in the whole district! We could see our name on the denomination's most important lists!

It was all there, that Sunday, building in my heart.

The "health and wealth" kettle was just beginning to whistle among us, and quickly building steam, and I was listening. A couple of people in our church were on the national TV program, "700 Club", for spectacular reasons. We had fifty men go to a men's conference, and in the big hot tub at Fairmont Hot Springs I baptized ten of them: in the middle of the night.

These are good things, but I wasn't thinking about each of those individuals. I was thinking about my doing it.

It's an occupational hazard in the ministry. Life and fame seem to be passing us by. It's looking like we really are going to die in a small Montana town and nobody will ever hear of us again. We are so blasted ordinary.

So we can want praise focused on *our* preeminence and not God's. When our goal of worship is to receive God's help to be successful, pride is taking over. Then we are just using God to further ourselves. Could it be that we now want church-growth secrets, or even God's Holy Spirit, for the wrong reasons? Have we slipped into a proud and competitive mode? Is this part of the reason why the American church seems crippled right now?

I sensed, that shattering Sunday, that this is what had happened to me. Oh, what a gut-wrenching moment.

What a hard period it ushered in.

I was reminded by the Lord that He was for the other churches in town too. In God's Kingdom our church was supposed to be for their good and health as well. I was to be praying for them, and helping them. I became so embarrassed after God convicted me that I apologized to another pastor in town for my attitudes that had benefited my church at his expense, and for my proud and arrogant spirit.

When his eyes suddenly teared up, I was both startled and even more ashamed. He said quietly,

"I wanted to say something to you, Miles, but you just wouldn't have heard."

What a monkey wrench humility throws into the gears of our pride! But God knows where to throw the wrench, and when he does, it knocks teeth from our gears, and everything slows down. But it needs to, doesn't it?

Chapter 14
MARYWOOD

It was December, 1984, and after checking in I sat down in my small room. I was at Marywood, a beautiful Catholic retreat center, situated on the edge of Cranbrook, British Columbia. Located in secluded woodlands, it offers a contemplative space in the shadow of the Canadian Rockies. The views of the Mountains of Fernie from its lounge and chapel are stunning.

After five hours of travel, I was here for four days of silence and solitude. Already I was out of my little town, my state, my country, my family, my denomination, my familiar theology. Talk about being "out of it": I thought several times,

"This is almost like dying!"

No one was in the center but me, and I had the chapel, the library, the lounge with fireplace, a special kitchen, and the whole sleeping wing to myself. It was Christmas time, and everyone else was scurrying around their churches getting ready for choirs, programs and parties. What perfect timing!

For me this was "Jesus Week"! I had dedicated the whole time to Him. So I sat down at the tiny desk in the Bishop's usual bedroom, and opened my Bible for my first "spiritual" time.

Amazingly enough, it wasn't ten seconds and an unpleasant face mystically rose from the pages and suddenly my Bible, the Bishop's room, even Marywood itself disappeared as I heatedly started to argue and even gesticulate while finally putting this guy in his place. The face belonged to Antonio Sanchez, a church member who had recently ragged on me with gusto! That distasteful Saturday evening he had come to the church while I was making final preparations for Sunday, and the tongue-lashing I received was an academy-award performance.

I feared, as we stood twelve inches away from one another, nose to nose, that he was about to have a cerebral hemorrhage. His manner was so heated and his face so red and hot that I tried to cool him down, as much for his sake as mine. It didn't work for quite a while, and I was at points frightened at being with him there alone. We weren't really alone, though we both thought we were. A young woman had entered the church and heard the angry voice. I say "voice" and not "voices" because I was frantically trying to defuse things, speaking quietly, because the Bible says, *"A soft answer turns away wrath!"* [21] That had worked once with my high-school basketball coach. It didn't work now.

This interchange, and other events happening right then, caused me to react strongly myself...at home of course...after the event...in my study downstairs...when I could say what I would like to have said if the Lord hadn't censored me. Karen just happened to overhear some of my frustrated outbursts, and then she said a life-changing thing:

"Miles, you simply must find some antidote to this inner poison, or you are going to destroy yourself."

Not long after that I heard about Marywood. It is owned by the Diocese of Nelson, and staffed by Sisters of the Congregation of Notre Dame, headquartered in Quebec. Pictures of Mary are everywhere, and I thought it ironic that I was here. Sister Nancy Hurren was to be my spiritual director. Direction from a Catholic Nun? I wouldn't say *that* to my fellow Assembly of God presbyters for awhile, believe me.

The week was absolutely wonderful after I stopped climbing the walls. It was amazing to me, though, all the horrible self-talk I heard in the quietness and stillness. Since I wasn't eating with people, or talking with anyone except Sister Nancy for an hour a day, I could now hear both myself and Christ much more clearly. I discovered that week why we like all our radios, TV's, computers, cellphones, iPods, newspapers, people, sports, hobbies, and activity. All that noise and busyness stuffs our conscious mind, and we can't hear much of what's incoming from God. And we can't hear, either, what's bubbling down there in our own subconscious.

"Miles...Miles!" said Jesus to me that night at the Bishop's desk.

"Where is all this crud coming from? Tony isn't here. Nobody is in this room but you and Me. I repeat, where does this horrible talk originate?"

I didn't need to answer. It was coming from me. It was the poison Karen referred to. And I was reminded it could kill me if I didn't find some antidote.

I did find my remedy that week. It was not a Scripture. It was not from Oswald Chambers in *My Utmost For His Highest*, my favorite devotional. I found it in *Christian Perfection*, a small book by Francois Fenelon, which I didn't find at Marywood. It was my own. I had brought it along, having just dabbled in it before.

Fenelon was a Catholic Bishop from the Court of Louis XIV who sought to live a life of deep and true spirituality in the middle of a court life notoriously profligate and difficult. Fenelon wasn't perfect by any means...as Luther, Calvin, and Zwingli weren't. All of them have some uncomplimentary, even ghastly, bits of personal history.

This Catholic bishop was *Catholic* and strongly disliked (putting it mildly) the Huguenots, some of my Pentecostal ancestors. But he was also a close friend of Madam Guyon, another saint of history, and both of them were widely misunderstood by their contemporaries because they loved "mysticism", which I interpret from my analysis as mostly a love of devotional insights and fervent faith.

Fenelon's last chapter, on *Humility*, just three and a half pages long, turned the rest of my life on its axis. After only a paragraph or two, I said aloud,

"Where is this guy from? Another planet?"

Immediately a strong thought filled my mind:

"Yes, he is from somewhere else... he's from heaven. What he is writing here describes the air and the atmosphere of that beatific place... it describes the makeup of the Trinity...their attitudes, the way they are...and the reason religious hotshots of history, who thought they did so commendably on earth, and cast out demons, and did such wonderful things in Jesus name, are going to be cast from him because they don't know Him at all."

Fenelon's chapter was all about submission and humility, the two main things Jesus said we are to learn from being yoked with Him.[22] (I know some translate *"I am meek..."* to be *"I am gentle..."*, but my own personal take is this: *"I am submissive...."*) Much of the church universal is shot through today, as I have been myself, with rank individualism, independence, and the virus of pride. God is the essence, however, and the fountainhead of both submission and humility.

Jesus said he came to do nothing on His own, but only what the Father wanted. We are to pray every day, *"Thy will be done, exactly as it is in heaven."* That takes more than gentleness. On some occasions, it takes white-knuckled obedience.

Fenelon spelled out both humility and submission, and illustrated them well in just three and a half pages. As I read it carefully several times, I felt the bubbling, sulfuric poison draining out of my heart. Listen to a snippet:

"Only Jesus Christ can give that true humility of heart which comes from him. It is born of the unction of his grace. It does not consist, as one imagines, in performing exterior acts of humility, although that is good, but (it consists) in keeping one's place. He who has a high opinion of himself is not truly humble. He who wants something for himself is no more so. But he who so completely forgets himself that he never thinks of self, who has no turning back on himself, who within is only lowliness, not wounded by anything...who does not affect forgetting self when he is all full of it...who is quite content to pass as being not humble at all; finally he who is full of (love) is really humble. He who does not seek his own interest, but the interest of God alone in time and for eternity, is humble." [23]

Oh, that I could quote the whole chapter! There are other things that spoke directly to me. Because of Fenelon I was prepared for 1985, a horrible year in many ways. For the next 11 months our board meetings would be chewed up with conflict and tension, much directed squarely at me. If I had not been prepared for the conflict by Fenelon, I would have detonated in January. But I had been forewarned and forearmed.

I went to Marywood for the next eighteen years, usually the first or second week of Advent. It was for only three full days there, but the drive north and the drive back south also became part of the silence and solitude, the contemplative event. Every year was special, but there were two that stood out: the first one I just recounted, and another where I was given a glimpse of heaven that remains vivid to this day.

I arrived that Monday night as usual, but noticed that I didn't have a surge protector for my computer. Fearful that I would damage my computer and lose years' worth of its memory, I went into downtown Cranbrook to find one. When I couldn't locate the store to which I had been directed, I stopped a couple strolling down the street.

"Pardon me..."

That was all I could say for a long, awkward moment, because after I spoke, they both turned and we were face to face. *I had never in my entire life seen a face as beautiful as that which now filled the world.* It was on the edge of human perfection, or the glimpse of an angel of God.

Please understand I have a ravishing wife. A man in our church once told me that Karen is the most beautiful woman he has ever seen, and he was telling me nothing new. I have been exceedingly graced by God to have her for my companion. We all know, however, that beauty is intangible, it is relative, it is everywhere, and no person has a lock on it. I am a normal man, and as such I delight, with most other men, in the beauty of the feminine side of human nature. But this woman was some cosmic *"Déjà Vu!"*

Looking back on it I can honestly say there was nothing sexual, nothing of lust in the moment, but only sudden shock and an absolute wonderment at God's stunning creation standing there. All I could see was the perfectly formed face, the large luminous eyes, the expectant look of a mythic figure. It was winter. She was in a full-length coat. All I could see was...that face. I have only seen one similar before or since, the face of a world-famous fashion model. But even the model's face is but a pale reflection of the transcendent memory in my mind.

After I found my surge protector, I immediately plugged in my finger...to protect my own circuits. The apparition's face was so compelling that it was never far from my consciousness the entire retreat.

"What is this all about?"

I wondered that aloud several times. I finally came up with the idea that God had given me a glimpse into heaven itself. Occasionally in life I have caught a soft breeze of that eternal spring, a flash of some coming delight, some stunning thought of what just might be in store for all who enter their eternal home.

I feel it is our privilege to anticipate that realm. The Scripture says, *"It has not entered into the heart or the mind of man, the things that God has prepared for those who love him."* [24] That should not keep us from trying, however, or keep us from noticing the subtle sightings that God occasionally grants.

On that forever-memorable evening, I glimpsed just one of the millions of faces that will be common on the heavenly boulevards. Gold there will be as common as asphalt here. So will beauty, in all directions. Every face will be transformed and improved, every countenance be aglow with the radiance of health and its own optimal promise. The best part of that magnificence will be that it radiates from within each person. After one breathless moment on a cold Canadian street, after just one glimpse of the future, I do not want to miss the glory that is coming.

I told the church about it the Sunday of my return. You can imagine the ribbing I received. But somehow my wife and the others understood that I had been granted a snippet of eternity, and I think it filled a few others with longing.

I was hoping for another sighting of the heavenly vision the next year, but on that visit the only unusual encounter was with a wild turkey. She came right up to the window of the chapel as I sat on the floor reading and listening to music. As we studied one another eye-to-eye, it wasn't quite as easy as the year before, but I still sensed some divinity in the moment.

That was Marywood every year: some new glimpse of reality, some good look again at myself, and some new vision of our Lord.

Chapter 15
MARK AND HANNELE

The tall good-looking Norwegian drove his pickup a second time, in as many weeks, northward along Highway 93. Mark Erickson was close to relatives in Ronan and that cheered him, but he was still traumatized from an attempted sexual assault the night before, made by two Hell's Angels in Great Falls, Montana. Mystified by the demonic violence, trying to understand the bestiality he had nearly experienced, he was questioning the reason for existence itself. As he drove slowly along he was in a deep depression.

"God, if you are really there, would you prove it to me somehow? Otherwise, I don't want to live."

At that exact moment a strong beam of sunlight broke through the heavy cloud layer covering the Mission valley and focused on Mark. It was enough of a sign: he "turned his life over" to Christ immediately. *Now* he understood what had happened two weeks earlier, just before he tried out the job in Great Falls.

On that previous occasion he had just come into Montana from California. Morally he was drifting because, thus far in life, in Minnesota as well as California, he and his brother Mike had been party animals. Locked into marijuana and alcohol and pretty girls, Mark was in the mood for more. He needed a party.

Right then he picked up a nineteen-year-old Hispanic with his thumb out. Robert Castro was from our church's youth group, the one led by a former Buddhist and her young Italian husband. Like the other eighty young people crammed into a tiny farm house every week, Robert had been fired up in his faith. Hitchhiking back to Polson as Mark drove by, Robert was on the lookout for another chance to share Christ.

"Wow," he thought as he climbed into the pickup, *"this guy's a candidate for conversion!"* He immediately said,

"Do you know Jesus?"

Mark said yes but inwardly thought, *"Duh! Doesn't everyone in this country know Jesus?"* Uncomfortable now with Robert, he switched subjects.

"Hey, Dude. Know of any party tonight?"

Robert at first didn't, but then he thought of Katie, a stunning teenager who was also in the church youth group. She was working at the Polson Chamber of Commerce booth. He guessed the two might like to meet.

"Not really," said Robert, *"...but I know someone who just might."*

"Party?" said Katie when Robert and Mark stopped by.

"Sorry. But I do know where there's a prayer meeting," she said with a cute twinkle in her eye. *"Try something different, Mark. Come with us to a prayer meeting!"*

He had never been to a prayer meeting in his life! The uniqueness of the idea, his total boredom, and Katie's unusual attractiveness persuaded him to give it a whirl.

"Why not?"

Mark was passionately drawn to a new love that night...but not with Katie as might be expected. (It was a mystery to all of us watching why these two did *not* connect. It sure wasn't Katie's fault. Her attraction for Mark had immediately flamed into strong love.)

No, that night Katie...and all girls...and marijuana and alcohol...and all parties...suddenly disappeared as Mark glimpsed things previously foreign to him: love for Christ...love for *prayer.* It was odd, even to him. He was suddenly blind to anything else.

He hadn't known of course, but Robert and Katie had made him a special target of their prayers, so just two weeks after that first youth meeting, and after that distasteful brush with the two Hell's Angels, and after one brilliant shaft of light through the clouds, Mark was a totally new person. Just like that! I swear it was that fast.

It was George Mueller of Bristol, England, all over again. About a century ago, Mueller...a hard-partying, hard-drinking, pagan Prussian...also visited a prayer meeting and was totally swept off *his* feet by a love for Christ and prayer. From then on, everything Muller did was to, in every way possible, bring honor and praise to God, especially through his praying. His life-long journaling had one main purpose: document how God answers prayer, and did he ever![25]

It couldn't have been more passionate with Muller than it was with Mark, and their beginnings in this whole dimension were almost exact duplicates. For both, their previous life patterns, the business expertise of their fathers and their parents' wealth...all disappeared in the mist of God's transcendence. Both were now consumed by God and prayer. They experienced the expulsive power of a new affection.

Mark soon joined Youth with a Mission (YWAM) and attended a new base in Bozeman, Montana, where he enrolled in a "DTS" (Discipleship Training School) and a "SOE" (School of Evangelism). It was exactly the training and the challenge he needed. His eyes were turned around in his head: previously focused only on himself, now he saw nothing but our sick world.

The political crisis right then happened to be the Pol Pot regime in Cambodia and the infamous "killing fields". Refugees were swarming by the thousands into camps just over the border in Thailand. In the main camp there were about 100,000 starving people.

Mark didn't look back. Believing fully in the power of prayer and in God's ability to provide, he said goodbye to Minnesota, California, Montana, his shocked parents, Katie and all other American young women.

He located a small Thai house on stilts in a village adjoining the teeming thousands in that main camp. Not worrying about disease or stone-age hardships, he started living like everyone else. And why bother raising support for this mission?

His wealthy Minnesota parents thought he had gone insane, and blamed some Montana fanatics for brainwashing their son. What a horrible *waste*! Mark could have been the president of a company like his father, been well-to-do himself in a short time. Why, against all common sense, would he throw his life away and become so altruistic? His father was beside himself with disappointment and anger.

Mark would not return to America for three years, and that was just for a short visit. He did live like the Cambodians. He learned the languages necessary. Daily, all day long, out loud, under his breath, with others, all alone…he prayed. For years on end. Even about the tiniest details.

Painfully, patiently he gained the trust and confidence of first this person and then that small group, eventually winning the admiration of the Christian pastors in the camp. Tragically these scores of various Christian leaders were avoiding one another, and even the desperate conditions didn't blunt their pride and competition.

This distressing fact slowly changed as Mark lived the Example and taught the Life, and eventually became the mentor of hundreds. He had time and thought and effort for nothing else but God, people and prayer, and God brought together a corps of Christian pastors that have since made historic strides for Christ in the new Cambodia, and throughout Asia.

Mark assumed that God wanted him to be single, that it would be cruel to ask a wife to live under his principles and conditions. But in the same camp there was a woman Mark's age, drawn there by the same motives and reasons; an attractive girl with whom Mark completely synchronized. She had come from Finland.

Hannele saw the possibilities for marriage long before Mark because he had given up any thought of that long ago. Finally, though, a deep love beyond friendship drew the two together. Side by side they served in that hellish camp of poverty and rejection and selfishness.

One by one and two by ten they reached people in Bible studies and through constant conversations, through teaching and preaching, touching pastors who had been locked in selfish competition. That healing radiated out to their little churches and to the unconverted.

Their first son was named Sophal after a godly Cambodian pastor friend. Gifts had poured in from around the world as the pregnancy advanced. It was thus tragic when the child died from complications during birth.

The anguished couple cried aloud,

"Why, God? WHY? We prayed so much before, during, and after this birth! We even prayed after Sophal's death for a resurrection. Why would you allow this?"

And God seemed to answer,

"Do you remember you also prayed for a deep empathy with these Cambodians about their suffering? Haven't you heard of the many family deaths and murderous horror that every family has experienced? Even now, after Sophal, do you really grasp the extent of suffering experienced by these people?"

They also learned the meaning of the name Sophal: *"The Seed that fell into the ground and brought forth much fruit."*

They had two more children in the squalor and filth, the dust and heat of the camp. Samuel and Paula thrived, however, as Hannele joyously mothered them.

But now *she* became ill. It was amoebic dysentery and it affected her heart, demanding skilled medical attention. They went to Finland. Mark was confident the medical interlude would be brief, but Hannele's heart arrhythmias had her bedfast, and in and out of hospitals for months. That meant Mark was the main parent to take care of the children. Samuel was two and Paula was six months. He was up and down all night and day warming the milk bottles, rocking them, changing diapers.

They lived with Hannele's parents, but since both of the parents worked, Mark was only spelled off in the early evenings. There was only time for a short walk filled with fervent prayer for his strength and his wife's healing. Oh, how much easier it was in the refugee camp! Back in Thailand he would get up to pray at 6 a.m. and work all day until 5 p.m., but it was never *this* hard. In Thailand Mark could never understand how Hannele would be so worn out from just taking care of two little babies. Now he knew!

Nor was there the same sense of accomplishment. No one ever said *"Well done! You did a good job with the kids today!"* He longed for those easier days of the refugee camp when he could see results. Now it seemed nothing but continual crying and dirty diapers.

Mothers everywhere will smile as they read of Mark's exhaustion and frustration during this period.

The medical leave stretched into years. Hannele, though terribly weakened by her illness, was finally able to maintain the home atmosphere and tend the children, even though she all but died several times from her dysentery. It was seven years before she was significantly healed in a special moment of God's grace. While visiting our home in 2008, Hannele's physical person revealed nothing of the brinkmanship and drama, the triumph involved in her story.

After Thailand, the Ericksons are in a whole new orbit: Finland, Sweden, other parts of Europe. Mark is fifty years old now and for thirty-two years, he has never lost his focus on the Lord and on prayer. He has prayer-walked the halls of parliament in Finland, prayer-walked the streets in many of Europe's cities, climbed his chosen and beloved "Prayer Mountains". Mark is always on-site somewhere, praying. China. Russia. The Ukraine. At one point he even traveled to South Korea, stretching his hands toward North Korea in prayer while walking along the border.

This story is not yet finished.

Mark himself got cancer. The ugly tumor wrapped around his heart and pressed down into his lungs, growing unchecked, and some Doctors were confident he would not pull through. Weren't Sophal's death, and Hannele's bad health, trials enough? The confusion returned.

As always, God had his higher purposes.

Before his cancer appeared, Mark had discovered that the Finnish pastors had as much dislike for one another as did those in Cambodia. With hostilities and betrayal tracing back through World Wars I and II, back through other hellish upheavals with Russia, many layers of outright hatred and suspicion had kept most churches and their leaders walled off from one another.

Mark, before his illness, had already fostered some reconciliation between these colleagues. Though these men still harbored resentment toward one another, they all loved Mark, and when his cancer struck, it became a powerful catalyst for unity. In 2008 there were pastors in twenty-eight cities working and praying together who never had before.

The cancer crisis built until all despaired it was Mark's last few days. In a final desperate attempt, his doctor prescribed a radical treatment that could have killed him. But it didn't! Not only did he survive, the cancer quickly shrank to scar tissue the size of a raisin.

Our man is back on his beat, adding significant teaching events to which the youth of Northern Europe are responding by the hundreds.

The Ericksons have begun a YWAM base in Finland. God led them to a public-school property that had been closed for health and maintenance reasons. With the broken pipes fixed, the windows triple-pane, the base paid for, they now have a rotating staff from many places in the world.

An outreach to Russian orphans has developed. In 1991 Samuel and Paula got caught up in praying for the street children of Russia who were sleeping in garbage cans. They not only prayed, she gave up her Barbie Dolls and he his Hot Wheels, and when the first ministering team from the base went to St. Petersburg, those toys touched the hearts of the children there as few things would.

One hundred Russian orphans at a time are now brought to nearby Finnish campgrounds for the novelty and fun of a trip out of Russia...and...for Mark's gentle but direct Christian teaching. In previous summers he was only given minutes, but each year now his teaching time is increased.

Just a few closing details:

In 2008 Mark was invited to New York to be the keynote speaker at a sizeable convention of Asian pastors, the very ones he brought together in the refugee camps of Cambodia.

Mark's brother Mike initially scoffed at his brother's turnaround, but after a death-defying close shave, an inexplicable near accident, he became a Christian too. As did Mark's mother and father.

Now the Ericksons are helping pioneer a second YWAM base in Finland. It's a beautiful old Hotel with fifty beds. Their own base has two main schools a year. Mark is an elder in a church, and still teaches in many locations around Europe. Samuel and Paula are doing very well.

Not much happens in Montana, which is just a suburb of Chicago?

Tell Mark that.

Chapter 16
DAN AND JACKIE

"What a JERK! That man is IMPOSSIBLE!"

My usually optimistic and accurate wife was steaming when I came home and asked how her counseling session had gone.

"I've rarely talked with a couple where I didn't think they could make it, but there's NO WAY that marriage is going to survive!"

We'd been so hopeful when Dan, at his wife's insistence, had agreed to marriage counseling with Karen. Stubborn Dan! Finally! Smoked out of his hole in Arlee, a community fifty miles away. He was the thirty-three-year-old husband of twenty-seven-year-old Jackie who had shown up on our church's doorstep over the last two years. We'd prayed for that guy the whole time. He absolutely refused to talk with any one in our church. We were a bunch of heretics. We weren't Catholics.

Jackie had been coming to a women's Bible study on Wednesday mornings, and showed up in the middle of worship each week, towing behind handsome little Nolan and gorgeous little Teagan. The relaxed, leisurely pace with which she entered the sanctuary, even at that late hour, the measured and kind way she herded her two little ones into the pew, showed in every move the relaxed grace of her Native-American heritage. The physical attractiveness radiating from all three of them spoke decidedly of French ancestry.

It was truly remarkable, the initiative and persistence Jackie showed by making it to church each Sunday. Living fifty miles away, she had to get up, at her peaceful pace, feed and dress the children, and then drive that long distance. We couldn't see how she did it.

Dan was a case study in the convoluted developmental patterns seen sometimes on the Salish-Kootenai Indian reservation. His family had minimal Native American influence, but Dan had enough of a tribal bloodline to qualify for tribal benefits. He had, however, a personal reaction against the welfare mentality that was quite prevalent, and he'd also picked up a strong work ethic from his parents. Though they drank socially, there was not the alcoholic dependence that damaged many long-term families on the reservation.

Good looking as Brad Pitt, Dan had no difficulty attracting girls. When they were just sixteen he and a girlfriend (not Jackie) conceived twins on their first intimate connection...a girl and a boy. Dan accepted his responsibility, made sure he was there for the delivery, and married the girl after the children came.

But the couple still loved partying and the bars, both of them continuing to date outside the marriage. They fought furiously over various issues, and after the children messed up their partying they worked out separate lifestyles. Dan placed all three of them on his parents; he felt his wife neglected the children. They both kept dating others, so they broke up. Dan did care for the twins as much as was possible for a working father.

Wouldn't you know...out of their mutual guilt the young couple reconciled for one day and a night. Whoopee! Here came another child. But twenty-four hours together again was enough for both, so they divorced. The wife got the little girl, and Dan the two boys.

One day Dan spotted gorgeous, "knock-'em-dead" Jackie walking down the street. She soon moved in with Dan, but it wasn't for long.

"What a JERK! This guy is impossible!" she quickly decided, just as his first wife had.

Now *she* was pregnant, and Dan's heart flooded again with good father feelings. He wanted to be there at the birth, be there for the child. Jackie didn't want him near her at all, however, so it took a platonic arrangement before she would live in the same house. The plan worked pragmatically for a long period, but she was adamant she just didn't like him.

He *was* to be her final answer, however. They did get married, as their first "fix" in the relationship. Dan vacated the party scene and the bars, because he didn't want to expose Jackie to the temptations he knew were always available there. All he saw in bars were people either dumping or being dumped.

Dan had started smoking marijuana when he was twelve years old, and this was always behind his domestic confusion. "Grass" was the first and the last thing he always bought with his money ...no matter what else they needed. Even so, he fiercely clung to his ideal of not being a sponge on anyone. He turned down a marvelous financial deal offered by his mother-in-law. She was ill and needed Jackie to be a caregiver, so she proposed selling them her house for just $2000. Dan insisted on paying his mother-in-law $35,000. Jackie couldn't understand why, but he needed to do that for his self-respect.

Not many of the "fixes" worked as they tried to steady their marriage. Marijuana still controlled the relationship. Jackie grew desperate, and that was when she discovered New Life Christian Center. She became convinced her sanity could be salvaged there, so she came, and cried, and talked. With us. With several others. With Blanche and Darrell Fried.

Ah, yes! Blanche and Darrell now enter this saga! Newcomers to our town from Great Falls, they had purchased the Carpenter Orchards after his retirement from teaching high school. They intended to enjoy a second lifetime of succulent Flathead cherries, apples, apricots, plums, and several other fruits from that storied orchard. Their new property dominated exclusive Hillcrest, just below the Lakeside Cemetery. It sat like a mother hen, fluffed over the Polson bowl and bay.

Talk about model Christians! Blanche herself had become a pastor after her first pastor-husband died of cancer. Alone now in her forties, she met Darrell who was also single again, having been rejected by his first wife. But the fact that he was divorced, however unfairly, meant that her ministerial credentials had to be terminated (according to our denomination) and so here they were, starting life over.

Blanche was a huge blessing from day one. Darrell was also a godsend. Wired with 220-volt energy, he not only managed his large fruit operation but also spread his gracious service over our congregational life. He was a wonderful Bible teacher for the adults. He was elected to the church board. He was there for special work projects and facility emergencies. I tell you: Blanche and Darrell were as valuable, generous and hospitable as all the original disciples put together. Well, almost.

And thus it was that Jackie and these two met and talked and prayed together. She wanted to end the marriage and let Dan grump to himself and smoke all the "grass" he wished. Blanche and Darrell listened to this litany of frustration time after time, but they kept encouraging her to stick with it and have faith and patience. Jackie would go back home and beg Dan,

"Please, Honey. Just come once to church with me. Come and see that it's not a bunch of wild-eyed kooks or heretics. Let's talk with Blanche and Darrel, or with Karen and Miles. I know someone up there can help us!"

But Dan's strong convictions and iron willpower would not allow it. Catholic from his jet-black hair to his toenails, he simply would not listen or budge one inch, and it finally became more than Jackie could take. Sinking into a serious depression, she had to *leave*, go *somewhere, anywhere.*

Ah! Blanche and Darrell's! They even had a place for her horse! And her pregnant dog! And Nolan and Teagan. They would let this happen *for free*, if she just wouldn't file for divorce. The Frieds saw good coming from separation, if Dan could thereby see himself better. Perhaps things would be knocked off dead center. Well, they certainly were!

It was at this point Karen counseled the couple, and it was a blowout.

"Dan...Jackie is about to self-destruct trying to relate to your teenage boys," she said. *" There seems to be bad blood between them right now. For the sake of your marriage, perhaps they should go live with their real mother."*

"WHAT? This stupid advice, coming from a minister's wife? What kind of a religious joint is this, where you would suggest something like that?"

It was not a good opening salvo! Even my cool and collected, wise and sensible wife came within inches of smacking the man.

Soon after that, Jackie moved into the Cherry Hill Motel in Polson. A day or two later the couple had their worst argument ever. Jackie convinced him she was through.

"Through, Dan! I'm through, through, THROUGH! GET OUT OF MY LIFE!"

As often happens, this experience of total desperation, this feeling of absolute helplessness was the turn-around moment. Dan dejectedly went home, buying a case of Budweiser as he went through Ronan. At home he watched his beloved NBA playoffs, whiffing down beers and yelling and cursing and damning New Life Christian Center to hell. It was mostly because we weren't *Catholics.*

He's been mystified ever since at what took place that night.

"It was truly a Saul of Tarsis moment!" he insists now. *"My heart was totally changed! I went to sleep a rank sinner. I woke up a new man! I can hardly believe it yet."*

Budweiser should make an ad about this! Or maybe the NBA.

Even though she had prayed for it, Jackie now refused to believe such a wild story. To her, Dan was just changing strategies, and being manipulative in a despicable way. To the Carpenter Orchards she went: kids, horse, pregnant dog and more.

Months went by. The dog had her eight puppies. Four-year-old Nolan fell in love with Darrell and they bought him a suit and tie just like Darrel's so he could strut at church and imitate his idol. But though Dan now talked constantly of his conversion, Jackie simply would not believe him. She actually didn't want it to be true because she *did not want him back*. She was convincingly resolute.

"I'm glad you're a Christian. But leave me alone anyway! Go and have a nice life."

But time, a softening in Dan, and especially Blanche and Darrell's wonderful caring and counsel finally won the day. Dan had laid down his bow and arrows and spear and hatchet, and was coming to Blanche and Darrell's home Bible Study. Their solid knowledge of Scripture, their gracious and kind explanations now made sense, for Dan was unusual in his reasoning, intelligence, and strength of conviction. All that really needed to happen was for him to read the Scriptures seriously himself and for him to give a fair hearing to the basic gospel. It was finally crystal clear... he *had* met Christ in a drunken stupor during an NBA playoff game while in a dead sleep. Who could ever script that?

Jackie finally accepted the authenticity of Dan's conversion. Not only that, she fell in love with him again, this time for good.

Overnight Dan turned toward the Lord and the Scriptures. Sharing with him became a high pleasure for all of us. He read voraciously, and even began to talk of Bible School to become a pastor. The Frieds were thrilled and offered to help toward his expenses when that plan worked out.

A new development postponed this treasured idea, though, and it had to do with the terribly important righting of the family's financial ship. They had been far from fiscal for a long time. To compound that problem, Dan quit his job of sixteen years because he realized it was a dead-end. Life became the scraping of any barrel within reach.

It helped that the whole family could live at the Frieds' as caretakers. A freak winter storm had frozen out the entire orchard. One very mild winter, a blast from Alaska hit, and in just ten minutes the temperature dropped sixty degrees. It was

"...bye-bye cherry industry" for several years. The Frieds had to sell their retirement dream.

God was with the young couple though, and one day a friend of Dan's, a man with no connection to the tribe, noticed a garbage disposal business was a possible venture if only Dan would serve as the door into lucrative contracts with the tribe. When Dan became a partner, it opened up financial opportunity, and finances have only been better since. The company built a fleet of trucks, and when Lake County shifted to a new garbage collection plan, Dan and his partners sold the company. Dan could still drive and earn excellent money. The couple could now afford new vehicles, a gentleman's farm of 13 acres, and five horses for Jackie. Young Nolan picked up her equestrian love and is now (get this!) an Indian cowboy.

Business was thus one thing that stopped Dan's being a pastor. The other thing was...family. Dan and Jackie became convinced they were not to limit their family's size. Because of this belief, they named their third child Jedediah, a Hebrew name for "God Knows!" They reasoned that God alone knew how large their family was to be.

They sure got that right, because Jackie gets pregnant every time Dan hangs his pants on the bedpost. We still don't know how far God is going with that bedpost. Delightful children just keep coming.

Moreover, they have proven to be the ideal parents. Not only does the large family not overwhelm them, they home school their children. Lindi, a mutual friend, came by our home once and shared what she had witnessed the night before: the family was sitting around the living room while the latest children were learning the Westminster Catechism. One by one they gave their answers to the long list of questions. The engaged father was listening intently. Lindi said it was beautiful. Jackie was sitting there, relaxed as always! *Relaxed*! With a family of eleven, including the three older step-children!

Do any of the siblings resent the regular additions? Obviously not. Jedediah, God's spokesman, told them he wants more, but since six of the eight are girls, he wants Dan to hang his pants on the other bedpost.

Jerk? Impossible? A marriage that would never make it? For once my wife was wrong!

Chapter 17
CHERYL AND JAMES

"Pastor, this is Cheryl," said the tearful voice. *"James and I need your help. It's bad."*

She gave her last name and I had no idea of what was coming because the two of them had come to church for the first time last Sunday. The memory of that event didn't help either.

"Miles," my secretary had informed me then, *"there's a new woman in the foyer asking a lot of people for money...for (sanitary napkins)."*

It had been Cheryl, and now, just two days later, I was suddenly her pastor, and she was in tears over some tragedy. I tentatively asked the reason.

"It's my niece, Katie. She wants her money, and we don't have any."

"Money for what?"

"She sold us some Girl Scout Cookies, and she wants her money, and we don't have it. We can't pay her, and she's angry."

"That seems simple: just give her back the cookies!"

"We can't. We ate them all."

"How many boxes of cookies are we talking about?"

"Fifty-two!"

As you might guess, Cheryl and James were both big-boned and heavy people. Once James told my daughter, Kim, that he had lost 25 pounds and weighed only 400 now.

"A man's got to think of his family, you know!" he said seriously.

Cheryl wasn't in that weight class, but she was pushing 250, so her exuberant hugs were soft and cushy.

It was people like Cheryl and James, those who were saddled with a rough life, who seemed to require much of my personal attention. Moreover, I never knew a time in our whole tenure when we didn't have wonderful people who were struggling somehow. But it is from that group that the best stories emerge; among them the grace of God shines.

Our interactions with these two, especially, were always interesting in the extreme and phone calls were frequent. I was once criticized for only catering to the medical doctors and bankers in our congregation. What a joke! If anyone got tiny amounts of my time, it was the upper-income people. If the critic only knew!

Many were the times, however, that Karen and I were grateful for our policy of seeing everyone as valuable to the Lord. Moreover, if people with big challenges came our way, He was in their coming. I was frequently frustrated about the hours chewed up by our more needy friends, and would sometimes wish I had more choice in counselees. But when the personality surprises were over, people like Cheryl and James often revealed hearts of gold, a true hunger for God, attractive winsomeness, and fun surprises.

There was one period of dedicated prayer in my time at Polson that I especially remember. I had called an early-morning prayer hour for men, and was hoping for a good number to attend. Concentrating on "contemplative prayer" at that time, the agenda was just to be silent together in structured solitude, and reflect only on the Lord. But James was the only one who showed up.

Daily, morning after morning for quite a period, the two of us met in the lower chapel and worshipped silently together. The Lord was truly sitting there with us during that daily watch, and it was there I sensed his deep pleasure with James. There was an artlessness, an honesty, a humor and winsomeness that was thoroughly enjoyable. James didn't have a job then...he never did...but that didn't matter. I was able to study the love of Christ for one special man. But something larger happened, too, much larger. I knew without doubt that it was God Himself sitting in that other chair. Looking at me. Loving me.

And they were hospitable.

"Hospitality", said George Macdonald, *"is a gift of the poor."* [26]

Does it seem to you that hospitality is scarce in the church now? Is it because we're all too rich? I recall one night when Cheryl and James had Karen and me over for pumpkin pie. Cheryl must have forgotten to put in sugar, and when pumpkin pie is not fixed right, it can look (and taste) like something else. Somehow we choked it down and chased it with coffee, enjoying the evening in their tiny apartment. We looked at their pictures, appreciated Cheryl's knick knacks, heard the latest about their colorful family members, and played with the new kitten.

Hospitality has taken on a different shape since I was a child. Perhaps it was our isolated location fifty miles from Miles City, Montana, but when people drove up in our yard, it was an event. We were honored at their coming, and my mother was expert at *"...throwing another potato in the pot."* With eleven people in our own household, it was a challenge to scare up more food on a wood cookstove, but my mother did it. When we invited people out to our ranch for various holidays the whole church was invited.

Later, moving into Miles City for public school, our home was still a magnet for people, especially on Sundays. If someone new was in church that day, my parents were often the ones who invited them over for dinner. My mother struggled with her deafness, but she functioned well enough that no one seemed to care. All their lives they were known by scores of people as "Mama and Papa Finch."

That whole attitude was carried over into our ministry. I did have to warn Karen before I invited someone, but on Sundays we usually had a roast in the oven because company for the Sunday meal was a given. That's when we could connect at a level otherwise not experienced, and with people who were often overlooked. Thanksgiving dinner was always a wonderful menagerie of strays from the church. And fun? It was sometimes wild.

The years took Cheryl and James a lot of different places. Unfortunately, they did divorce, and James moved back to California. Cheryl and her children remained in our general area, though, and she was always enthusiastically connected to some local church fellowship.

During one of our visits back to the church after we'd retired, Cheryl rushed through the foyer, threw her arms around us, and once again called us Mom and Dad. There was no self-consciousness as she crushed us against her pillowy bosom. It felt so good!

But it was while the choir sang that we fell in love with Cheryl all over again. It was Christmastime, and there she was in the large choir, on the right side, standing out like a Christmas tree, for in her hair she had a passel of multi-colored blinking lights. It was Christmas, for goodness sake. And Cheryl, as usual, knew how to enjoy church, have fun, and celebrate her faith!

Chapter 18
FRANCIS AND JIM CHAPIN

The widow Francis Chapin was definitely losing ground. During recent sermons she muttered back at me, and it wasn't a whisper but something people could hear three pews away.

"Get it SAID, for crying out loud!"

Encouraging things like that.

Francis had been among us for years by this time. It was getting towards the end of her mobility, her mental lucidity, and when she could remain at her home. By now she was wobbling into church on very high heels, even in wintertime. Her makeup was askew and heavily plastered on, and she smelled up the whole area around her because of her chain smoking.

Definitely pretty in her prime, that beauty slipped further away while we watched. At first she had hints of the earlier attractiveness she had flounced around husband Jim's insurance office: the fine facial features and the heavy head of hair, the classic figure. In winter she wore fur coats, and jewels and hats. But more and more we had to do mental gymnastics to reconstruct a true vision of the past. Her photographs at home definitely helped.

For quite a while after she began attending our church, I couldn't compute her past and present relationship with Jim. The marriage was more muddy than usual. Pastoral ministry regularly delivers fascinating living puzzles, and that fact was part of my work's enjoyment.

My, but the endless variety! None of us have the same nose, for instance. And that helped me in relating to the wild assortment of individuals God sent our way. Since God cares about each of us enough to give us a unique nose, then why would we ever expect him to rubber stamp our other parts, especially our spiritual development?

Jim and Francis were coarse, and swore freely. In hoarse smoker's voices they freely threw out evangelical and Pentecostal phrases, and tantalized me with the mystery of their background. After several visits they finally revealed they had been married in a large Assembly of God church in a mid-western state by a prominent minister. He had once spoken at our Montana Glacier Bible Camp.

I kept visiting them at home, feeling like a toy mouse being batted around by a couple of old bored cats. Each visit I felt they were more amused at my naivety than interested in any perspectives I might have. They had always been there and done that. They knew my lingo, and not much about our denomination was a surprise. It was frustrating and fascinating at the same time.

I'd start a concept, a spiritual or discussion thought, and just a few sentences into it, Francis would jump in and finish my sentences and bump the conversation off track. Then Jim would disagree with her, giving a secular or confused theological twist to her comment, and they usually ended up shouting at one another. Every time I stumbled out of their house I vowed not to go back, but something (Someone?) kept pulling me into their vortex.

Finally Jim came to church with Francis. He only came that once because that next week he discovered he had cancer. You would think that would give him an existential kick toward recommitment, but it didn't work that way.

I began visiting them every week, and I was aiming at some kind of spiritual change on his part, perhaps even a first-time conversion. After a couple of months of this regularity, Karen said one day,

"Miles, you mean to say that you have gone there every week for months, and you can't get Jim to respond to Christ? What's going on?"

"Hey, do you want to try? Why don't you go next week and give it a whirl?"

"OK. I'll do that. This is getting ridiculous."

So next week Karen tried her hand at the conversion of Jim Chapin.

"My word! What kind of fish is that on your wall? It's huge!"

"Blue Marlin. Caught it in Florida on one trip we took."

She eased into the conversation with general questions and observations.

"I think I'll go into the kitchen and fix some refreshments," said Francis.

It was a good idea. As usual, she kept sticking in her two cents' worth about everything. With Francis supposedly gone, Karen moved closer to her main intent.

"So, Jim, this cancer thing must be quite a concern to you, right?"

"Yeah, it's for damn sure not something I would choose."

Cautiously Karen tried various approaches to spiritual things, but she was getting a good taste of my problems. From the kitchen Francis would still jump into the conversation at any point that had promise. And when Francis jumped in, Jim would clam up and get angry, so Karen had to start all over again. That happened repeatedly for a solid hour.

With a splitting headache by this time, Karen got to her feet.

"Jim, my goodness! I've been here an hour already. I'm sorry. I'd best be going. You look pretty tired, and I'll bet you'd like a nap."

"Well, it is getting about that time, all right. Here, let me walk you to the door."

"No, Jim, you just stay right there. I can let myself out just fine."

"I will walk you to the door. I appreciate your coming, I really do."

So they walked to the front door together, Francis not interrupting now, and at the threshold, Karen didn't quite know what to say, so she just blurted out:

"Jim, whatever you do, don't let anyone come in here and try to convert you!"

"I can't believe you said that!"

"I can't believe it either."

So ended my wife's attempt at saving Jim. When she got home it was dinner time, and I was there.

"Well, how did it go? Did Jim give his heart to Christ?"

"Yup! It was as simple as could be. I can't understand your problem, Miles."

"Aw, c'mon! NO! You're pulling my leg. Now tell me, what actually happened!"

She admitted her failure and felt that she had probably ruined everything. We commiserated over the whole impossible situation and pooled our ignorance on what to do next. Deciding

I would just keep my regular weekly schedule, we would pray harder and wait for something new to happen. On my next visit, Jim demonstrated a new openness and relaxed manner that indicated the games were over. Our relationship took on a new honesty, a fresh tone.

Jim got worse, and it was now very serious. There was a real conundrum developing because our vacation was a week away, and we wanted to attend a C. S. Lewis Symposium in Seattle. But it seemed that was the week Jim would likely die.

I went over a day or so before we had to leave, had a great time with Jim, a warm and close time that I concluded with a penitent's prayer of commitment which included Romans 10: 9-10, emphasizing that Jesus was *OUR* Lord and that *WE* believed in our heart that Christ was raised from the dead.

"And Lord, you promised that on the basis of these two confessions of faith, we would be saved! Saved from sin. Saved from death and hell. Raised into eternal life. Thank you for those wonderful promises, Lord."

When I said *"Amen!"* Jim joined me with a loud *"AMEN!"* of his own. My heart leaped. There was force in that Amen. Commitment. Let it be written and so let it be done, was in that *"AMEN!"*

Next, I explained the situation and my dilemma.

"Jim, I don't know what to do. We have planned a trip to Seattle right now, but you seem to be in very serious condition and could die while we're away. I don't want to be gone at that moment, so I'm canceling this trip."

"Oh, you go to Seattle, Miles. I'll be fine, really. Whatever happens, I'll be fine!"

Then he clasped my hand warmly and said,

"Goodbye, Brother!"

Brother? He called me *"BROTHER?"* Somehow in the warmth of that one word and his strong *"AMEN!"* earlier, I knew everything was okay. His eyes were soft and shining, his manner relaxed and serene. The cat was out of the bag. He knew that I knew he was right with the Lord.

My, but do I ever dislike "squeakers" like his conversion, though.

We did go to Seattle. And Jim did die two days into the symposium. I drove back to Montana for the funeral, leaving Karen in Seattle as Francis insisted. The widow was relaxed and in charge, confident and the center of attention.

Francis was able to stay in her home by the golf course for about two more years, after which she had to move to the convalescent center just across the street from the church. Bonnie Allred and I were very involved in regular visitation, as was Sylvia Vandeberg.

To her end Francis was often cryptic and acerbic. Her speech was still peppered with profanity. She was furious when she was not allowed to go to her house.

It was difficult with Francis, as it had been with Jim, to evaluate her standing with God. At the end there was a softening, and more response to prayer and Scripture. But it was another occasion for me to commit a dying person to the grace and mercy of God. I console myself this way: my information is horribly incomplete; God's grace will be revealed as beyond comprehension; our future life is filled with rapid growth in all areas; and our main enemies here – the world, the flesh, and the devil – will no longer impede. We will all recover lost (or previously ungained) ground quickly.

Yes, Jim's three daughters were there for the graveside ceremony, which is all they wished. Francis was "the other woman" who took their dad from their mother. For that, her step-daughters had disliked her passionately, and angrily avoided her and Jim.

Francis signed over the house to them, and there was some measure of reconciliation and healing involved in that.

She gave $28,000 to the church.

I got something out of the deal, too: an aluminum extension ladder I still have.

And Bonnie Allred got her fur coat, which reeked from Francis' smoking.

Oh! One more thing! Remember that pastor in the southern state, nationally known in our denomination, the one that wowed everybody at our Montana camp meeting? He was stripped of his ordination because of adultery. It happened when Francis and Jim were going there, and when they were close friends with him.

That's the rest of the story. The spiritual battering and disillusionment they went through because of that Pastor helped explain many things. It explained their wide repertoire of evangelical and Pentecostal catch phrases. It explained their wariness with me. It helped explain their profane coarseness and their slow re-ascent into faith and new commitment.

But they made it back, Praise God! It may have only been by the skin of their yellow teeth, but they finally made it back into faith.

Chapter 19
HE WAS A "JAVERT"

"Javert" (Jah-vair) was the hard-nosed lawman in Victor Hugo's play, LES MISERABLES.

For years he pursued Jean Valjean because, to Javert, Valjean only deserved

to be in prison (for stealing bread to feed his sister's children).

Law was law. Rules were rules.

And grace was just too unthinkable, forgiveness too hard.

Many in our congregation are native Montanans, and for one period of time some of us were almost in Nirvana, the time when the state had no speed limit. Traveling long distances on our straight interstate highways just begged for the European speeds of the autobahn. Our highways are better than that storied system, as is obvious to anyone who has traveled on both. And many of us who had cars engineered to do 105 mph in fourth gear (not fifth) loved it.

One heavenly day I was driving ninety-five mph in fifth gear (just loping along) up the East side of the Bozeman pass in my 1986 Audi. The sky was blue, the springtime mountains were green, I didn't have to keep an eye on my backside, and the driving pleasure was immense. It was pleasure, that is, until I was passed by a Toyota Tercel, their "pocket rocket", their smallest car. Going uphill.

Our congregation always ribbed me about speeding, but some of those hypocrites drove faster than I did. And when the speed was left to the driver's discretion, they couldn't really complain. But the good days didn't last, as they never do. The state reinstituted speed limits.

Wouldn't you know, I had the added misfortune of having both the local Chief of Police *and* the area's Montana Highway Patrol's Sergeant in my congregation. Ron Buzzard, the police chief, carefully watched me in town, and Barry the Highway Sergeant had all eight of the area's patrolmen peeling their eyes for a certain pastor.

I was alerted by my brother in Great Falls before Barry came to town:

"I hear you're going to have a wonderful family move to Polson and to your church. They have attended our church here for years, are the church's youth leaders, and Barry and Brianna are just wonderful! They have the three cutest little daughters, and he's a wonderful speaker. Oh, another thing: he's a highway patrolman!"

"Aarrgh! Not that," I groaned.

Barry and his family did indeed prove to be a blessing. He was one of those guys whose every sentence is funny and he made full use of the hilarious experiences he seemed to have every day at work. Arrested people can be very humorous, and Barry wove his stories seamlessly into his teachings and conversations. And when it came to humor, Brianna could keep up with him.

Moreover, they had a heart for the youth group of our church, which grew in numbers immediately.

But Barry was a lawman, a sergeant. All joking aside, I wouldn't have gotten much mercy had he ever caught me speeding which, amazingly, he never did! Laws were laws and rules were rules, and pastors and Christian young people had better understand that.

"If I catch you speeding," he told me more than once, *"you'll pay your fine!"*

Once he pulled over our attractive church secretary, Jeanie Brenneman. I happened to drive by, rolled down the window and said,

"Throw the book at her!" He did.

Law and grace clashes mightily in youth work, and it certainly did at our state's youth convention one year. Along with our group that particular time was a youth who knew how to push every wrong button in adults. Tension built between him and Barry over several infractions during the first day of the trip, and Barry tried to tighten his grip on the young man's behavior.

But he had met his match. This kid was an expert in manipulation and deviousness, and it all came to a head as the two of them finally had it out. Standing by an automobile, it was possible for Barry to utilize his police-force training and spread-eagle the youth over the car hood. Cranked up (and clanked up) by the youth's maddening pleasure in the conflict, Barry did just that. It was time to emphasize law over grace, which Barry did, adding something like:

"You young punk! Mess with me, will you? I'll teach you a thing or two!"

The group consultation with the parents and Barry, after the convention, was interesting in the extreme. The father was a person totally sold on love and grace and flexible understanding of his son. Barry was just as convinced of the need for law and rules and obedience and consequences. The classic struggle of the ages, law and grace, was thus played to a standstill yet again as the two sides came to loggerheads. No understanding whatever emerged between Barry and the parents. It was obvious to me that both parties needed to listen and learn, but it just didn't happen.

Well, the boy obviously did need a lot more control than he received, for the succeeding years were a deepening spiral of disappointments and discipline. I think every possible state program was tried with that young man. Blessed with good looks and a huge appearance of promise, he was proving the adage: *some promising young men only become promising old men.* (Happily, he is now married and doing much better.)

This was a real crisis for Sergeant Barry. It injected a note of anger and irritation in him that kept deepening. It curbed the enjoyment he had in youth ministry. Even his pleasure in the Christian life diminished dangerously. It came to the point where his wife had to assume the leadership of the youth group. Fortunately, they still made a good team. Barry reduced his involvement and was basically there to assist in...discipline.

The Scripture says, *"See to it that no one fail to obtain the grace of God; that no 'root of bitterness' spring up and cause trouble, and by it the many become defiled, that no one (becomes) immoral or irreligious...."* [27] It is a warning with many layers of consequence: we can block God's grace to ourselves; bitterness can take over; troubles can come; many can be defiled; becoming immoral is possible; abandonment of the Christian life is not unthinkable. Suicide can even happen as a result of this legalistic blindness and frustration.

How is all this possible for good people? But it is! Barry entered a period of spiritual disintegration from which we all feared he might not recover. He became humorless, or his humor became biting; he withdrew from both the church and his family; he then had a torrid affair with a female law officer (which he confessed, to his credit). At his wife's insistence, he moved out of his home and into a low-rent apartment where he slept on the floor. It was a very hard experience for all of us and so sad.

His wife and girls were marvelous through the ordeal. She continued with the youth work and was very honest with the young people, who were supportive prayer partners. It was an assignment for all in the church: the application of law and grace, faith and works, morality and gospel.

I was so proud of our people! No one stormed in and demanded that Brianna stop leading the youth. No one urged that we discipline Barry by removing him totally from membership. (He *was* moved to inactive status during that time.) Chris Bumgarner reached out to Barry, and I assume others went by his apartment just to show love and caring or give opportunity for conversation.

And my dear wife: she took Barry on as a special assignment, in prayer and practicality.

"Barry, come over every Friday evening for a good meal!" she urged.

"Oh, I can't do that!" he objected. *"You don't really want me to come over."*

"Yes we do! Please! You must be on a horrible diet these days."

She used the fine china and silverware. The food was the best. And he came, honestly saying that it was for the food. During the meals we just talked.

Karen, wise but strong as usual, honestly addressed the issues. (He seemed to be much more open to her than to me.) She acknowledged the elephant in the room (his whole set of problems), but she did it with beauty and grace as well as strength. It didn't go totally unheeded. Barry labeled her *"A Pit Bull in a Pink Ribbon"*.

But he still continued in his bitterness and adultery.

If we had ever wondered about the superiority of grace over law, this experience with Barry illustrated the ultimate power of grace. Gradually it worked its miracle in both Barry and in his family.

Grace? Brianna certainly had to exercise it, and that was how we counseled her. She was being advised by many to divorce him, *"...throw the book at him,"* get on with her life, and she did have justification for that direction. She could have walked away without guilt and started a new life. Their three girls were also pulled into the whirlwind and struggled hard with anger and bitterness, but they watched their mother and learned about new levels of love.

It was grace, grace, grace, from every direction. And it finally got through to the tough lawman. He couldn't believe the reactions to him from Brianna, his children, the youth group, the church membership and board.

In sequence, he stopped his affair, tearfully confessed his sin publicly in the church, asked our forgiveness and specifically that of his family, and thanked his wife profusely and publicly for her forgiveness.

That Sunday morning Barry and Brianna stood together in the pulpit and shared their journey. The congregation was breathless, especially when she said:

"Barry was actually very close to suicide. I found his briefcase and opened it, I guess at God's prompting. It contained a suicide note, instructions as to who to call, and a loaded revolver."

Barry was *that* close to validating Victor Hugo's characterization of Javert. The proud lawman of the novel, *Les Miserables,* committed suicide when he couldn't humble himself, couldn't accept Valjean's sparing his life, and was so legalistic about law that he couldn't forgive himself. Interestingly, that's the very reason Barry gave for the planned suicide: Law was law. If he couldn't forgive others, why should he forgive himself?

It was a new man speaking now, a new man leading the youth group. Barry was restored to his former youth pastor position, and he reflected in all things his radical change of perspective.

He has, in fact, changed careers.

He is now the pastor of a strong church in a nice Montana town. Totally honest with that pastoral-search committee, he found them so moved in the first interview that they cried right along with him. And there was no hesitation...they wanted him to be their spiritual leader!

Is grace more powerful than law? It's one of humanity's biggest questions. Our church saw it convincingly answered.

Chapter 20
MALCOLM AND MARIA

The beautiful young woman with two small children stood transfixed, watching. It was the first baptism by immersion she had ever seen, and she had been in church all her life. Her mother was a hard-core Italian Catholic, and would have been furious to see her daughter in our church that day. But Maria's attention, with small Mark and smaller Melvin pressing tightly against her, was riveted on the drama that depicted the death of our sinful life and resurrection into Christ. For her, the symbolism was brand new!

"Could I meet with you sometime this week, Pastor?"

I was still standing in the water as we talked. Our baptismal area was floor level in the dining room of the church so it would prompt dim images a casual riverside setting. We agreed to meet.

"I just left my husband in Bellingham, Washington," she said on Thursday. *"I didn't know where else to go. Along with my brother, we own a place on Whiskey Bay."*

"*Do you have a cabin on your property?*" I asked.

"*No. We're staying in a tent.*"

"*How did you happen to visit our church Sunday?*"

"*Well, that morning I needed worship and church very much, but I didn't know where to go. So I just jabbed my finger at the phone book, and it landed on New Life Christian Center. I thought, 'I love that name! New life! Do I ever need that! Can it ever be possible again?'*"

The moment she walked into our foyer, she sensed she was home.

"*I cried all the way through the service!*" she said. "*I couldn't help myself, but strangely, they weren't tears of sadness. They were tears of joy. I've never had an experience like that before.*"

We often observed that with visitors as the Spirit of God moved on them through the hour of worship: happy, healing tears, a glimmer of hope in a life of confusion and darkness.

"*I learned this week that my husband was not only having an affair with one woman...but with two, and the second was my best friend! Here we were, going to counseling in a church and I thought we were making progress. But last Wednesday all of this exploded in my face again, and I just couldn't take it.*"

She'd quit her job in Seattle and left with flaming eyes, in humiliation, and with intense resolve. It was over, this marriage.

But Malcolm actually did love his wife and boys. Trapped by the power of sin, however, as all of us are by nature, he was himself baffled by his actions.

"*Damn, why can't I help myself?*" he wondered. "*Why am I treating her like this? I love her and the boys. I don't want to lose my family.*"

He knew how outstanding and talented, how beautiful inside and out, how fun and humorous Maria was! He just thought he could keep her and party on the side.

So it wasn't but a few days and Malcolm showed up. He talked for hours with me, with Karen, and with good men in the church. He cried and apologized and stumbled all over himself for weeks as he shuttled back and forth to Bellingham where he was involved in real estate development. I was impressed with him in many ways. He seemed sincere in his repentance and contrition. He prayed the sinner's prayer, read what he was given, and admitted to his adultery. Maria gladly and wholeheartedly let him back into her life.

But Sandra, Maria's main other competitor, was by no means going to release him without a fight. It was war now, and she ratcheted up her vast skills. Malcolm capitulated whenever he went back to Washington. Eventually the facts became known because Sandra herself let Maria know with a triumphant sneer over the phone.

"He doesn't love you, Maria. He loves ME! He's sworn that to me over and over! This week!"

Maria disintegrated, and she feared for her life this time, so she checked into an area hospital for help over the first critical days. Now it really was over! The feelings at church, the returning hope, the Christian talk and promise…it all seemed a cruel joke. She ripped their wedding picture into a score of pieces.

But with one last feeble grasp at hope, she kept the pieces.

Malcolm was now so motivated to change things that he decided to move to Polson also, and start a new contracting business. The one in Bellingham was dying, legs straight up. Zoning laws had stopped all activity there, and they couldn't even sell the lots. They were deep in debt and all their years of financial success were disappearing in Washington's coastal fog.

They were both remarkable in their work history.

Malcolm had started with some entry-level position at the Merrill-Lynch stock brokerage in Seattle. But his drive, ability and skill took him to both the Florida office of Merrill-Lynch where he was working deals with the wealthiest, and also to the New York office on various important assignments.

Maria, for her part, was a genius at computers. At the time she left Seattle she was the main computer problem-solver, teacher and consultant at a very large insurance company in Seattle, one that had the top eight floors in a downtown skyscraper, and offices in eight other states. She was responsible for the functioning and programming of over 2000 computers.

Why was Malcolm now in contracting in Bellingham? Well, it wasn't just another attempt at leverage and advancement. It was the women in Florida and in New York. All those thongs and bikinis on bicycles in Florida drove him wild with lust, and the attractive people he worked with every day in both cities added daily to the distraction. Corporate parties deliberately excluded spouses so both Malcolm and Maria agreed this job was just too dangerous.

Maria had no idea how dangerous! Many of those women had been more than a distraction. That all came out as he came clean. In this new attempt at reconciliation and repentance, he did get serious. He called me and four other men together and confessed it all. It wasn't just two adulteries. You would be shocked at the number. He knew all the secrets of male subtlety, subterfuge and seduction, and had put his knowledge to work.

But Sandy, back in Bellingham also knew the sexual craft, and she became a Tasmanian devil. She called him every day in Montana, and hounded him from job to job, phone to phone. With a black belt in manipulation and having a near-fatal attraction, she had his mind in shreds, to say nothing of Maria's.

Maria didn't let Malcolm move back into her house this time. She realized the enormity of the problem, and his betrayal was just too great to surmount without something miraculous and convincing, without solid proof over time. So what did we do?

For starters, I let Malcolm sleep in a church office. Next, Sandra had to route all of her calls and threats and sneaky ideas through my wife and me. Malcolm had to meet regularly with a group of men who hounded him with accountability and questions. And they both talked much with Jerry and Linda Praetzel who have a very effective seminar named "Plumbline," showing people how to line up their lives with Scripture. In our society the Praetzels often find that their seminar deals with sexual puzzles.

Eventually Malcolm was allowed back with his family. He had demonstrated that Sandra was out of his life. He had severed all the business commitments in Washington he could. He had proven his contrition and repentance. The thing that seemed to break the back of his demonic bondage was that confession to five men. Coming to the light, bringing it all out in the open, worked exactly as Jesus said it would.[28]

Prayer helped as well, and exorcism. Faithfulness at worship, and regularity with his accountability group...all assisted in the change. So we had a renewal of vows and a service of Christian remarriage. The wedding picture was pieced back together, and placed in their home hallway. The year was 1996.

The redemption continued with almost breath-taking speed. The couple, as I mentioned, was on the brink of financial ruin, with huge debts and property that couldn't be sold. But Jesus said, *"Behold, I make all things new!"* Could any of us believe Him for that in this circumstance?

Malcolm and Maria heard about tithing and supporting God's work for the first time. And they started obeying immediately, even while bouncing on their financial bottoms. God must have loved it, for the money mess mysteriously started to untangle.

One day Maria got a call from Seattle.

"Maria, is there any way at all you can help us? Our main computer guy in Milwaukee just quit, and we are really left in a mess. Can you go there for three weeks?"

"Oh, I just don't know. I would need a good wage."

"Maria, we were paying this guy $100 per hour."

So Maria agreed to a good wage, and left for three weeks, working ten and twelve hour days. After that, they needed her for three more months. This time she got more money yet, and insisted that the firm bring her family along. They found themselves in an expensive condo right on Lake Michigan.

It was "win-win" every direction they looked. Their lots in Bremerton sold. Their bank account mushroomed. Malcolm and his sons were able to spend unlimited time together, bonding better than ever before. The boy's deep distrust and hurt was diminished, and healing in them now began.

Soon after Milwaukee they made a successful bid on an older but nice Polson home on Hillcrest Drive overlooking Flathead Lake. Malcolm got into the real-estate appraisal field. He has become a wonderful Christian man, husband, father, businessman and church member. Highly respected in the church, he was elected to two terms on the board while I was pastor, and always served with distinction. He is a wonderful conversationalist, and his influence keeps growing.

After his conversion and recovery, in a letter to all affected friends and family members, Malcolm wrote this moving account:

"...I (eventually) found myself in a room with five other men confessing every sin that came into my mind...everything, no matter how ugly the sin, came out. Boy, it was exhausting, but you would not believe the freedom I felt. The joy that came over me can't be described. What is crazy is this: here I am, feeling this incredible joy at a time in my life when I had a six-figure unsecured debt, a so-so job, no home and my wife told me we were done for good. Yet I am happier than I had ever been in my entire life. On that day...my lust...died! The memories of that evening of confession will give me joy forever. Yes, we still face the typical trials that life brings everyone, but I don't go deep end when they happen and I realize how important even a little Godly tenderizing can be."

Malcolm has met faithfully with the other men for the years since. They require confession of the smallest of sins in this, their weak area. And now Malcolm is helping other men climb out of their similar hell. Even men back in Bellingham.

Maria? She has been able to become the stay-at-home mother she wanted to be, and also a marvelous vendor of grace in the whole community. Loaded with crackling wit and intelligence, she spices up every contact with humor and her wonderful laugh.

Maria's staunchly Catholic mother? She came to love our church almost as much as her own, and became a bridge of understanding and grace between the two congregations. Most importantly, through all of this horrendous treatment of her daughter by Malcolm, she was kind, gracious and forgiving to him. Just before she died, the two of them experienced great warmth and tenderness. This, when *she had lost her own husband to unfaithfulness, abandonment and adultery.* He left her because of the physical effects of her stroke. She and the children experienced a long life of single-parenthood, near-penury, and large trials!

Sandra, the Tasmanian she-devil? Ten years later, she was still calling anyone she could locate with her devious desire for contact with Malcolm. As C.S. Lewis wrote, *"When you sup with the devil, you'd better use a long spoon."*

Mark, the older boy, is graduating this year, 2009, from a university in California.

When he was just three years old, Melvin was delivered, through exorcism and special prayer, from a frightening manifestation of his father's previous bondage. We are not talking usual childhood experience here. His leering lust appeared out of nowhere and was expressed in adult words, manner and force. It was as if a literal spirit had fastened on him, the same one that nearly destroyed his father. Evidence does suggest that evils like this can become a trans-generational curse. Scripture says that the sins of the fathers can be passed on for generations. But in Melvin's case, after prayer and a word of command, it simply disappeared. His parents have not seen any symptoms since we prayed. Now Melvin absolutely loves his church youth activities and regularly won first place on a Bible Quiz team.

I wish Harry had been able to watch this story unfold.

(Remember Harry? The guy in the restaurant who thought churches were leeches on society?)

Chapter 21
"TRUST JESUS!"

"Do you ever counsel someone who is not part of your church?"

He was hesitant, hard to hear.

"I've gotten myself into a lot of trouble, and I need to talk. I thought a pastor might be the place to start. My name is Howard."

"I'd love to meet with you, Howard, but I'm unavailable for a couple of weeks. Would that be soon enough?"

"I'm willing to wait."

He had indeed destroyed his life. A high school custodian for years in a near-by community, some serious criminal activity was exposed, and from then on his life unraveled within weeks. He was arraigned and waiting for the court system to work through attorney appointments, time delays, and court appearances, but was still released "on his own recognizance". Needing money and something to do in the interim, he found a job with a cleaning company in Kalispell, fifty-five miles away. His Uncle Jake extended a helping hand, so he did have a place to stay during the devastating wait.

He had signed over his power of attorney to his second wife in a moment of guilt and rash impulse. Understandably furious at him, she immediately started using her new legal power to transfer or sell absolutely all of his life's assets...new Dodge Ram pickup, nice 37 foot trailer house, tractor, Bobcat excavator, expensive tools of all kinds, treasured things from his father, even his last pickup, which was a ratty old Dodge D-50. The value of everything at the time was probably $250,000.

Wife number one was a different story. She was a strong evangelical Christian (he remained deliberately clueless) and she was the one who reared their three attractive daughters to internalize the faith. Howard was a trucker during that time, away from home a great deal, and dominated by his inner turmoil. He was the one who ended that marriage, realizing the bad home environment he had created. Even though his wife still loved him and didn't want a divorce, Howard pushed it through, and found wife number two in a bar somewhere.

The suffocating truth of his predicament settled over him more every day as he drove to and from Kalispell. It plagued all his thoughts. He came to feel there was no way out of this one, and started planning his suicide as he ground through his hours. Having decided he would do it by going up into the mountains and deliberately freezing himself to death, he was dejectedly driving Highway 93 one day, twenty miles from Polson, when a small, flopping, letter-sized, plastic-coated sheet of paper caught his eye. It was tacked to a power pole 100 feet from the highway.

"TRUST JESUS!" was its simple advice.

He looked at it daily as he drove by, disregarding it, but on the tenth day he suddenly started sobbing so much after seeing it he had to stop the car for several minutes.

"I guess that's one thing I haven't tried," Howard said as he fought for control. *"Maybe I'd better talk to a priest or a pastor before I actually do this."*

So he started calling priests and pastors in the area, and tried to determine from their words and voices alone if *"...this were the one or not."* He called four as he began his search, but each time he simply hung up after only hearing them answer the phone. He said nothing to them, answered none of their questions. Just hung up.

"I couldn't feel any of them was the right guy."

On the fifth try he dialed my number. For some reason he immediately felt comfortable, and told me he found himself in double-trouble and needed some priest or pastor. Two weeks later we connected.

I have never seen a more despondent, vacant face. As he dribbled out sketchy details I could identify with him, speak the language, and offer hope for change. I suggested a commitment to Christ, the basic Christian mystery: *"Christ in you, the hope of Glory."* [29] Without the divine life inside a person, true Christian change is impossible. View it this way: if a dead person is on the floor, you can bark out orders, yell, kick, lift or violently jerk, and it's all futile effort. But if that person has even a sliver of physical life, he can respond. That's also true in the spiritual dimension.

Jesus counsels, *"Look at me. I stand at the door. I knock. If you hear me call and open the door, I'll come right in and sit down to supper with you."* [30]

The genius of Christianity is Christ Himself inside us. When He "comes in" a whole new life-principle is activated and life can turn right-side-up in moments. Remember Alan the trucker? Our first step to dealing with all evil within is a simple prayer: *"Jesus! Please come in!"* It's as simple as that, and as profound as that. That's why I'm a pastor today and not a psychologist.

Howard got it and prayed a simple prayer as I led the way. He started reading the Bible and other things I assigned, was baptized, and started talking about his change.

When I checked the accuracy of his story, Howard asked:

"Do you remember you gave me a Billy Graham booklet on forgiveness? Through that pamphlet I saw I needed to forgive myself. God could forgive me, but if I didn't, I was still locked into my hell. When I grasped that Christ loved me, I was able to love myself again. Can you imagine how important that was? After what I did? It was a huge breakthrough!"

Something else that helped Howard was exorcism. Evil is not a conditioned reflex, not speculation, but malevolence personified. Sometimes evil is a literal personality from hell that needs to be evicted. We need help with that, so one evening Jim Haynal, Dan Brander and I commanded the demons harassing Howard to leave. He suddenly started chanting,

"I'm protected by the blood of Christ! I'm protected by the blood of Christ!"

Where did that come from? I hadn't put the words in his mouth.

Howard was, from then on, more different still.

As was right, his conversion didn't stop the grinding gears of justice. He ended up in the Montana State Prison for thirty months. His description of the experience might surprise some.

"How free I felt in prison. Freer than I ever did on the 'outside.' It served as a kind of monastery for me. I can see why some prisoners get 'institutionalized.' It can be for good reasons."

Most who are sent to prison hate every minute and want everyone else there to do so too. Once I worked a "Cursillo" in the old Montana prison, and the first warning they gave us was never to whistle. No one is to enjoy being there. One big difference between a prison and a monastery is that the monks are glad they are there. And Howard was a monk.

He actually experienced much kindness. No one ever showed him disrespect. He had special privileges. Prison regulations stated only two books per cell: Howard had 150. He had access to a computer, and even had a small office in the chemical dependency department. He was allowed to work more than usual, and learned college algebra. He even taught some classes.

We communicated faithfully. I went to see him occasionally, and he attended weekly worship and Bible classes and took his programs of disciplinary treatment. He wrote everything down in diaries and notebooks. Part of his motivation came from watching fellow prisoners. Some would do nothing but sleep all day, every day, for months. Noticing this type of person particularly, he said to himself,

"I don't want to leave here brain dead!"

When the parole board interviewed him, one of his supervisors (who had not read a single thing Howard had written) said, *"If I was (sic) you, I would waive my parole possibility because you know what people like me think about people like you."*

Another psychologist, though, was impressed with this particular prisoner, and sent the board a glowing report. So did I, as did Howard's three lovely daughters. It worked. His cynical supervisor and the letters from Howard's second wife were disregarded.

I came to pick him up the day of his release, and it was fun to watch. He huffed and puffed up the steep sidewalk toward the last double-lockdown with a two-wheeled cart stacked high. The guards said it was the most stuff they'd ever seen anyone cart out, and I believe it. I could hardly get it in my car.

In order to be released he had to have a home on the "outside", and also a job. So we asked him to live with us, I found him a job, and sold him my Mazda pickup. He lived with Karen and me for six months. There was absolutely nothing left of his previous considerable assets. He left prison with the $100 they gave him, and that was it!

It seems horrible injustice, really. According to Howard, the court-appointed public defender in Polson was to deposit half of the money from several big-ticket items in an escrow account for Howard's use after prison. This lawyer instead gave it to his wife to deposit. She deposited it all right. Somewhere out of sight. He never saw his rightful part again.

Howard views it as the hand of God pruning away his past.

Perhaps you are asking why Karen and I would invite a person with this particular propensity into our home when it was now just Karen and me living alone? Well, true to my impulsive nature, I had suggested this to Howard one day while visiting him in Deer Lodge. Karen was shocked and nervous about my offer, my children angry and uncomfortable because they didn't know Howard at all, and others were irritated with me, too. Of course I was ready to back out.

But Karen prayed about the idea and felt God was in this after all, so we allowed the plan to proceed. It did seem that he was worth the risk. I had scores of long letters from him in my file, and he kept all of my replies. He had tried his very best. When we talked, there was enough of God's revelation coming through that we picked up sincerity and reality.

Karen reminds me occasionally that Howard, during his first time in our church, saw an "aura" around me. But he also saw a much brighter one around her. He was thus primed to listen to her more than me, and the two had significant conversations while he lived with us. Karen has always been perceptive and wise, strong in faith, and rooted in Scripture and prayer. He and she would talk through things and Howard has remarked since about the value of those conversations.

After six months it seemed right for him to be on his own, so he bought a tiny motor home and continued rebuilding his life.

It was tough. He was a lonely man. He was afraid that, at fifty-eight years old, he would be branded worthless, even dangerous, and automatically discarded as marriage material. But an attractive Christian lady, fifteen years his junior, began to notice him. They met at "Twelve Steps for Christians" in our church basement. After a couple of years, after pooling their penury, after careful prayer and consideration, and after she dyed his hair, Spring married Howard.

Now it was tough for two, mostly because of finances. Their combined pile of debt was huge. She'd been left with a financial mess by her ex and owed $30,000. They debated bankruptcy but their hearts wouldn't approve, so Howard worked any odd jobs he could, and Spring continued in the excellent position she had at an area hospital. Watching pennies, they hoped someday to buy a house and fix it up, but it seemed they were locked forever into renting. Looking on, I despaired.

Karen and I, upon retirement, made final repairs to our Polson home before selling, and we had one thing left to do in the garage. A man named George was working there already and I asked Howard to join him in completing our project. As the two talked, the subject came up that George was leaving his wonderful caretaker's position, and his boss was looking for someone at retirement age with wide-ranging maintenance skill.

They had talked once before, but Howard had been working on a move to Oregon and thought it wasn't what he wanted. But this time when George mentioned it, Howard and Spring decided to check it out.

The job is absolutely ideal for his strength, skills, and desires. Both of them witty and fun, Howard and his boss are fast friends and really like each other. Howard told his new employer right up front about his history, and that was wise.

The location is truthfully one of the most beautiful on all of Flathead Lake. Forty feet away in a bay are swans, Canadian geese, ducks, coots, and wild birds of all kinds. The caretaker's house is new, a generous three-bedroom, with a two-stall garage. They have new furniture, their debts are getting paid, and everything he gets to do is fun. Howard again has a very nice, nearly-new Dodge Ram pickup complete with camper.

Do you wonder about his first wife and his beautiful daughters from three lifetimes ago?

The first week Howard woke up in prison, he etched his inmate number onto his electric razor (which he gave to me after his release). Also that first week, his three beautiful daughters drove the 650 miles from Tacoma, Washington, to reaffirm their father. They did it several times during his imprisonment. After his release, when he could leave Montana with permission, Karen and I followed him through Tacoma to meet all of them at the house of his lovely first wife and her husband. It was a wonderful experience. Grandpa Howard no longer has any need for suicide.

It was just a flopping sheet of paper on a power pole: *"Trust Jesus!"*

Chapter 22
JIM AND TERRI

After the benediction I darted through the offices and hall to the foyer, wanting to meet the new couple. Everyone in a small church knows when someone new is present, especially someone not the norm or beyond their group's stereotypes, and this couple qualified. Both taller than ordinary, they had listened intently through the service, more than usual. That level of attention is always refreshing, and I wanted more contact if possible. They seemed, well, Presbyterian.

"What are they doing here?" I wondered.

I caught them right at the door. Trying to be warm and welcoming but showing a poorly-disguised inquisitiveness, I said,

"Nice to have you with us today! From this area? I don't think I've seen either of you before."

Stock questions. But the return body language and attitude was very emphatic:

"Bud, you're not looking me over. I'm looking you over!"

Jim didn't say it, but he didn't need to. This guy didn't want small talk or a slap on the back. He even seemed a bit irritated I caught him before leaving. He had come. He had seen. He was out of there. On his first visit earlier, when I happened to be in the hospital, he had said to the greeter,

"I know you are very glad to see me, but I just may not come back!"

Terri was warmer but also maintained distance. I got the point: I shouldn't probe for any more information. When they were gone I assumed they didn't care for me, or us, and we wouldn't see them again. This happened occasionally. Our church was not seen by some as a blue-chip company. It wasn't where you went to socialize or line up business contacts. If you checked out a church like ours...chances were good that you might be desperate.

I didn't know it, but they *were* desperate...and so intentional that they visited every church in Polson, and some in Kalispell fifty miles away.

Months later I was shocked to see them again. This time their attitude was different. Jim wasn't as grim and gritty. Terri was more relaxed. They stayed for the coffee hour, and they were there the next Sunday, too. Weekly I began to hear the quick and wonderful laughs they both had, and not just theirs. Anyone around them was usually laughing, too.

One Sunday I asked, *"Jim, would you like to go with me to a men's retreat?"*

"Where?"

"Up at Glacier Bible Camp in Hungry Horse. The men of Kalispell Christian Center are putting on a big retreat, and they've invited our church men to join them."

"Count me in!"

We both expected several men from our church to attend, but at departure time it was just the two of us. Jim suddenly saw this as providential: now in A.A., he was at the point where he was to do his "fifth step", which states:

"Admitted to God, to ourselves, and to another human being the exact nature of our wrongs."

He asked his A.A. sponsor how he would know the person with whom he should share such personal material.

"Oh, you'll know. Someday a person will pop up in front of you, and you'll sense he's the guy."

Jim sensed I was to be his fifth-step person.

The retreat was wonderful. We roomed together, and he started revealing himself rather quickly...and...it was fascinating!

He had just finished an alcohol-detoxification program at St. Pat's Hospital in Missoula, one costing him $10,000. His drinking had reached the stage where he nipped all day long at his home-construction locations, and he had bottles stashed everywhere: at home, in his boat, under the hood of his pickup, behind its seat, in his toolbox. He was starting to black out, have times of really disturbing disconnectedness. So he decided to check in at St. Patrick's Hospital in Missoula to regain some control over this thing. He didn't want to stop, just dry out a bit and back up a few notches so his drinking wouldn't be such a problem.

In the month-long program, however, the first thing was a physical exam, and the diagnosis was that he could die if he ever took another drink. That thought alone sobered him, so he tended to business for the month's therapy, and got a wonderful start in the A.A. principles and program.

But nearing fifty now, he also wanted to reconnect somehow, somewhere, with his Christian background.

"I had wonderful Christian parents," he said. *"And we were in a very good Presbyterian church. I did listen and learn. After high school I got a basketball scholarship from Westmont, a liberal-arts college which required Bible and theology classes.*

"During the whole four years, though, I lived two starkly different lives. During the day I was the model Christian, but all night long I partied...hard. The college administration eventually learned of my hypocrisy in my senior year. After a lot of debate they bent the rules and I was placed on probation until I graduated. I just learned to cover my tracks better because I was already hooked on alcohol."

It was no wonder his body was at its terminus when he entered detox.

One night after college, Jim met Terri at a bar.

"He was my ideal!" she enthused. *"Here was as funny a person as I'd ever met...always the center and life of the party. But he could also talk about God and serious things with depth and clarity. I'd never had anything to do with church myself, but I had a lot of questions, and he could answer so many of them. This was my guy!"*

Jim had been looking for Terri. She could match him joke for joke, laugh for laugh, drink for drink. It was during the sixties, so they partied all around California in tie-dyed shirts, long hair, and a homemade Diamond T truck motor home. The floor of that contraption was a mile off the ground. Thus began their years of endless booze and belly laughs.

Moving to Montana, Jim decided he wanted to try building a log home. He had never done it before, but was so gifted that soon he had his own company and contracts galore for homes of real distinction in the Bitterroot valley.

It wasn't many years and they could afford a place in heaven... beautiful Polson on Flathead Lake. Jim and Terri built a unique log home right on the Flathead River, just above Kerr dam. With his powerful ski boat and her beautiful flower gardens, their place was party central.

This life collapsed. In addition to Jim's increasing dysfunction at work, Terri was secretly juggling the finances, frantically trying to satisfy all the creditors.

They were now ready for radical solutions. The fancy boat trucked down the road first. Then the nice camper and the two new pickups. Finally the beautiful home on the river. I'm getting ahead of myself here, but...God approved. In an unusual way He led them to a brand-new home in Jette Meadows, one better suited to their new life.

Didn't Terri like alcohol too? Yes, she matched Jim drink for drink but for some reason she didn't fit the classic picture of "alcoholic". When Jim stopped for his treatment, she also decided to stop. She did it without difficulty and without withdrawal, without temptation or remorse, without paying anyone $10,000. She just quit!

It was a high privilege when I baptized Jim and Terri one Sunday after worship. They had found their peace in Christ, their home in our church, and were radiant as they emerged from their virtual Jordan River.

I have seldom seen more involved participants. He shoveled snow, set up tables, ran crews on church workdays, helped at our men's retreats.

She volunteered everywhere she could.

He and I met daily over a long period to pray together at 7:30am right after his early-morning A.A. meeting downtown. (Note the time! When did this guy get up? Early, believe me, and he had his personal devotions before he went to A.A.) We'd pray in a back pew, or go up on the hill by the TV relays while looking over our little white settlement on an Indian reservation. What a marvelous person to also help me by prayer and encouragement.

One day he asked,

"Miles, do you think Terri and I could start a 'Twelve Steps for Christians' group in the church? We'd pay our expenses and take care of all our reading materials. Tuesdays would be just great! We'd run it like A.A., but be more open about its Christian roots."

"What a terrific idea!"

It has continued for years. Scores of people have been helped to understand the marvelous principles of Alcoholics Anonymous, and also been drawn closer to Christ.

Participants have been guided into local churches, including ours. In a recent baptismal service, three-fourths of the candidates came out of that Tuesday night group. There's actually a second church there...within the primary church building. And Jim and Terri are its lay pastors.

What so distinguishes this couple is their phenomenal servanthood. The last step of the A.A. twelve-step program is the joyful action of giving, of service. If an A.A. member has received help through the first eleven steps, he/she is now to channel that knowledge and gratitude into practical acts of love every day, every week.

No one could ever do it better...at home, at church, at the early morning A.A. group. Someone need a helping hand to move? Call Jim in the evening, and the next morning he will have seven men from AA there helping the stranded and snowed-in newcomer to town.

Dinners at their home. Bible studies there. Sponsoring new A.A. members. Jim, serving on the church board. Terri, running a support group for women that have had cancer (because she is since a survivor). The genius of this couple is that they understand and apply the A.A. principles to every kind of setting.

The bulk of Christians do not even know A.A. is founded on principles from Christianity. Each of the twelve steps is dug out of the Bible and is a careful adaptation of that principle which should never have been abandoned.

Take the "anonymous" part. It is a curtsy to church custom for Jim and Terri to let me use their real names, but note the absence here of a last name. A.A. sees the terrible liability and destructiveness that comes from the pride and ego-centricity of pushing success stories. They deliberately work against puffery and prominence in each meeting and, indeed, the whole movement. When I see the way pride has so riddled the Christian movement, I wonder how we can continue to be so blind.

Can you believe the self-important displays on some Christian TV programs? Each church has its people who can slip into conceit, including the pastor. (Oh, how I know!) This not only saddens the aware observer, but it can sow the potential for moral failure and scandal. Christ didn't live or minister like this! And he warned constantly about pride.

A.A. refuses to sensationalize or advertise around personality and flashiness. And where did they get it? From the Bible. That goes for all the twelve steps.

Look at Step Four: *"Made a fearless moral inventory...."* Know what that means? Radical confession. Sitting down and scouring our past lives for all the rotten things we have done, writing them down, telling it all to some sponsor, or friend, and then making amends as far as can be done.

The Bible counsels, *"Confess your faults one to another that you might be healed."* [31] Do we see much of this in the Christian church today? We act as if sin doesn't even exist, let alone confess it. Or we think we can go off in a private corner with Jesus and adequately deal with our past.

I grieve that I grasped this so late in my life. I wish the whole of Christianity would do a new and extensive study of A.A.'s twelve-steps, and apply them to the faith.

Jim and Terri are still right in there, serving and blessing others. The present pastor can't believe his good fortune at inheriting such people.

Five years after my retirement, at my seventieth birthday party, 200 people hooted and howled as Jim and Barry the baker roasted me in a skit worthy of prime-time television. Guess who was in the kitchen, pinch-hitting for the caterer who was called away at the last minute? Terri.

"Bud, you're not looking <u>me</u> over. I'm looking <u>you</u> over."

Am I ever glad I made the cut!

Chapter 23
JOHN DOWDALL

The letter read in Rotary one Tuesday was a bolt out of the blue. It had come the previous week to the club's president, and he read it aloud. It was from John Dowdall, one of our favorite Rotarians. Every St. Paddy's day he would sing in his wonderful tenor voice some Irish song like *"Tim Finnigan's Wake"*, or spin some Irish yarn, or recite an Irish verse. He had an infectious laugh. Everyone loved John, and John loved everyone back.

As one of the town's leading citizens he helped found First Citizen's Bank, the only locally-owned bank for many years. He was chosen for important local committees and started some of our most successful community promotions, such as "Port Polson Ahoy". He and his bank worked with the Salish and Kootenai Tribes to build KwaTaqNuk Resort, the nicest convention facility in the Mission valley.

Just before retirement he led the promotion and financial drive for our new hospital. A staunch patriot and veteran, he spoke all over the state at various Veteran's Day celebrations.

Polson's summer theatre building is named after him because of his strong promotion. The list of his accomplishments and plaudits goes on and on.

So it was a treat to have John write us from his new home in Arizona. He was sending a verbal bouquet to both the club and individuals within it. He affirmed first this man and then that man, and every person mentioned beamed with pleasure at the kind words and the jokes.

My chin hit the floor, though, along with the rest of the club, when he wrote a significant portion of his letter to...me. John was one of the most significant Catholics in town. He came from Anaconda and Butte, hard-core Catholic country, and was called back there every year for several of their biggest church and community events. And here he was, in this letter, saying I played a real part in his spiritual life. At one point he warmly labeled me "Father Miles". At that designation, several in the club looked at me with astonishment. I could almost hear them thinking:

"What is behind these strange comments?"

Label a Protestant, and a Pentecostal at that, a *"Father"*, a *priest* in your life?

Most of the Rotarians didn't know that John and I and a few others met weekly for twenty-seven years for a 6:30 a.m. prayer breakfast. We migrated to different restaurants, but it began in 1973 at The Goode Ship Lollipop. John happened to be there, and liked the dynamics. A group of us kept up the routine and some "founders" still meet every Saturday: Oliver Dupuis, Ralph Campbell, Richard Best and Bob Strong.

John was there every week he found it possible. We went through Oswald Chamber's book, *My Utmost For His Highest!"* four times at least. We would read the page for that day and relevant topics always emerged. We prayed together. We laughed together: My, but did we laugh! John's presence guaranteed that. I often wondered what other patrons at the Driftwood Restaurant said when they heard the chuckles and snorts from a *Bible study!*

One day I was talking with two Catholic priests, and the local priest at the moment introduced me this way,

"Oh, by the way, let me introduce you to someone from my parish: Harry, this is Miles Finch."

Did the guy know what he was saying? What *was* he saying? The introduction rankled me immediately, and I hoped that it didn't show. What chutzpa! I was part of *his* parish?

I've since looked up the definition and have thought better of the statement. When someone pastors in a community, all are part of his parish, even the other pastors. What he does, what she says, who that pastor *is*, affects everyone in the community. And the longer one is there, the more of the community he "pastors". She becomes a local fixture, he becomes an institution and a mile-marker for, if nothing else, how old everyone has become.

I always enjoyed the interdenominational contact. How boring the church would be if we were all the same! What colors, what distinctions, what wonderful perspectives come from other Christians who see things differently! That was one reason I always supported the ministerial association, even though it had every possible stripe of pastor there could be. Rank fundamentalists. Rank liberals. The highly intelligent and interesting. Those not so swift. Pentecostals like myself who sometimes embarrassed us. Actually, over the years it seemed that every denomination took its turn making us blush.

So we had a monthly ecumenical forum of sorts. I say "of sorts" because we didn't get much theology decided. Mostly we discussed the transients coming through town, or the food pantry with its latest successes, squabbles, or inefficiencies. Yearly we would coordinate a Good Friday service, a combined Easter Sunrise celebration, or a Christmas concert.

But substantive theological discussions? A combined Christian voice in the community? I guess so. Sometimes. Not as often or as completely as I wished, but there was always a solid collegiality and camaraderie between a few of us at least. With those guys and gals I always saw myself at the end of a long collection of Christian extension cords, starting at the main receptacle, Jesus. I loved it.[32]

Hence, I loved being with John Dowdall, preeminent Catholic layman. With him the Christian dialogue was always superb. I was deeply saddened once when a mutual friend suddenly turned sour on the Catholics. Throw every Catholic out of God's Kingdom? Throw out John Dowdall...who loved Jesus (it seemed to me) more passionately than many Christians I knew? Listening to John in his church as he shared...from memory... long scriptures from the Gospel or the Epistles was an *event*. He always did it with such joy! Throw him out, too?

If it's said the Catholics are wrong on this or that, I ask: Which of our groups has everything Christian and spiritual exactly right? Who of us would be so foolish as to think the devil hasn't messed up our group in some fashion, and used us to blacken the name of Christ?

Jesus once talked about a farmer who sowed good wheat in his field.[33] But when the crop came up, there was a distressing amount of wild oats scattered everywhere. His hired hands seemed more surprised than he was about it. They were ready to rip out that damned darnel and burn it in hell-fire immediately. But the farmer (God) said to just let it be. An enemy had sown all this crappy seed in the fields of Christianity. It was sad, but it wasn't the end of the world. When *that* event came around, *then* would come the time for serious sorting, and angels would get the honors.

We should all live by conviction. But we should also live in humility. We do that by sincerely admitting that we, too, have foreign ingredients in our special Christian recipes. The "field" in which the enemy sowed bad seed isn't just one religion or one Christian denomination, but in them all. He sows wild oats in all the "wheat" of the world; in politics, education, economics, other nations and world religions.

And he sows it in our own individual hearts. Sometimes what's sown is harmless. At other times it's very destructive. But *all* of us have foreign matter in our churches...and weeds in our lives. It's baffling. It's saddening and angering. We don't really know what to do about it but...wait...wait for what is really good to mature...and wait for the angels to come and do their thing with the weeds.

John Dowdall is dead now, but one thing I know: he's in God's wheat bin. And I hope...oh, how I hope to God...that I'm placed in that same bin in heaven. He's one of my best friends. I say *"IS"* my best friend, because he is not really dead, according to Jesus. In spirit he is up there somewhere, poking a Pope's funny bone, slapping St. Patrick on the back, learning another Irish joke, or just helping prepare some part of heaven for the rest of us.

See you later, John. And thank you for the verbal-bouquet at Rotary. I've never had one nicer.

Chapter 24
RELINQUISHMENT

I had never enjoyed preaching more, and feedback reflected the congregation was still profiting. Most things for me personally were going well. But in September of 2002 a member observed,

"Miles, I don't understand it. We have a wonderful facility. In my estimation, your preaching is excellent. We have outstanding people. There are just a lot of things going right in this church. I can't figure out why we're not growing."

Thoughts about the prophet Jonah somehow sprang to my mind.

"I think I know why. It's me, my friend. It's time to throw me out of the boat."

"What do you mean? No. That can't be it. That's not possible."

It was more than possible! In the days following, thoughts about our conversation crowded my mind:

"Why did I respond with that observation so quickly? Was God in that thought?"

"Perhaps several people are asking his questions."

"A new pastoral equation would be appealing. This church needs a new adventure."

"And it needs additional staff, but I can't add them now because, by our denomination's laws, they would have to resign when I resign. Such disruption for them would not show integrity on my part. It's best if a new pastor can start with a clean slate."

"Face it, Miles. You can't pastor here indefinitely."

I know Advent is considered the start of a church year, but September always felt more like that to me. By July the liturgical church year had built to its crescendos of Easter and Pentecost. School was out for the summer, sports programs had cranked up conscripting our young people and several adults, and I welcomed the lazy days of summer.

Church camps were available. Every week brought a reunion of some kind to town, with its visitors from the past and from afar.

But when September came the street bordering our church campus was gridlocked because the Middle and High Schools were next-door neighbors. Life clamored anew with rejuvenated fall schedules. Every year I felt ready, and was eager to begin again.

But in 2002 my engine didn't want to start. Could I last another year? Only Karen knew my thinking, but she felt the same. We wondered aloud to each other:

"Is this it? Is this the time to resign?"

We made a pact to pray about this for three months. I made one list of reasons why I should continue, and another why I should resign. We recalled that the Chinese writer Watchman Nee wrote something applicable. To condense and paraphrase him:

"There are only two principles of conduct in the world. The first is the principle of right and wrong. Most of the world goes by that. Many non-

Christians agonize more about rightness or wrongness than Christians do, but the Christian principle of guidance is different. It is the principle of 'Life'. Ask: 'Do I feel a quickening of life as I contemplate this word, this action, this decision, or do I feel a languishing of spirit?'"

It's an intuitive or mystical approach to guidance, of course, but we felt this *can* be what the New Testament calls *"...being guided by the Holy Spirit."* We had both experienced this quickening (or languishing) before, and noted this inner voice can be pithy. In fact, aren't lives changed more by sentences than sermons? I've sometimes said during Sunday worship,

"Listen for that sentence today that can change your life!"

Jesus castigated religious types who would pray long prayers, thinking they would be heard for their many words. *"Just say 'Yes' or 'No',"* He once urged. *"Anything more than that comes of evil."*

His "sentence" to me finally came in December. I walked into my study that morning, and as I put my knuckles randomly on my desk, this came full-blown to mind:

"Miles, it is one thing to throw away a gift of God, and it is quite another to relinquish it."

I didn't know what to make of that.

"Do you mean that if I resign I would be throwing away the gift this church has been to me all across the years?"

Was he telling me that?

"No, this time you would not be 'throwing my gift away.' You have wanted to do that many times in moments of anger, frustration, boredom, temptation, and fear. Remember?"

Did I ever!

There was one period when I felt like selling the church to the school district for a couple of million. Other ministries by the score needed money, so why not oblige them generously for once? Was I ever tempted to throw away the gift of God? Yes!

The Lord continued:

"Though you felt like it, you didn't. You knew that wasn't my will. But now I want you to relinquish this ministry, relinquish these people and this place, and relinquish the comfort and predictability. Your time here is over. This church does need new energy, new adventure, new and fresh vision... and that means a new pastor."

A wise friend lived nearby. Karen and I arranged to discuss our situation with him and his wife. That night we talked about our prayer vigil, our feelings, and I read my lists of why I should or shouldn't continue, and also mentioned the abrupt thought I had in my office. My friend said,

"Miles, it's clear the word from God is 'relinquishment'."

His wife agreed. Further conversation only underscored this impression.

So in January of 2003 I announced our intention to resign at the end of June. We would serve until then to give the church board and a pastoral search committee time to get their bearing and some direction. We notified our denomination's state leaders that they were now guiding and supervising this transition. We would only be caretakers for a few months.

I had not tried to groom anyone to take my place. I looked that direction once, and talked with a bright young man several times about the possibility, but the more I talked, the more I felt it wrong for me to make this decision for the church, for me to try to control their choice. They were mature enough to handle this on their own.

They jumped at the chance. Sensing God's will, the church board accepted their assignments with undisguised excitement. This church was no longer "mine" in any sense, as it never had been: it was the Lord's and theirs.

Ahhhhh! Relinquishment! My resignation sermon's title. It felt so good!

"We die daily. Happy are those who daily come to life as well," said George Macdonald. Beyond each death (relinquishment) is a new and larger resurrection. After our releasing one of God's gifts, another is placed in our hands, which we can also release sometime.

God confirmed our resignation in two very special ways. In the first, Ruth Aden called and said, *"Karen, there's a scripture that I feel applies to you and Miles somehow, but I don't know what to make of it. It is 2 Kings 25:27-30."*

> "And in the thirty-seventh year of the exile of Jehoiachin king of Judah, in the twelfth month, on the twenty-seventh day of the month, Evil-merodach king of Babylon, in the year that he began to reign, graciously freed Jehoiachin king of Judah from prison; and he spoke kindly to him, and gave him a seat above the seats of the kings who were with him in Babylon. So Jehoiachin put off his prison garments. And every day of his life he dined regularly at the king's table; and for his allowance, a regular allowance was given him by the king, every day a portion, as long as he lived."

We seldom saw ourselves in a prison or in an exile (Did a time or two!), but Ruth's scripture was spot on about the timing of our change: I retired on exactly the 27th day of the 12th month of our 37th year.

We noted the 2 Kings passage said we would dine*"...every day of our lives...regularly...at the king's table,"* and also that our King would give us*"... a regular allowance, every day a portion, as long as we lived."*

That has proven to be true, far beyond our hopes and calculations.

God's second confirmation of our retirement's rightness was the pastor who replaced us, and his preparation for coming to Polson. The day I informed the church of my decision, I said,

"Dear, dear friends: Remember that my resignation in no way takes God by surprise. Somewhere, for a long time, God has been preparing your new leader."

That statement was so true. Eight years earlier, now-pastor Shawn Madsen had driven through Polson and God whispered,

"Someday you will pastor the church here."

The thought came with such force he even called a friend and documented the incident.

While we served in our interim capacity, several new people started migrating our direction. The increase continued while seminar-leader Jerry Praetzel and his wife, Linda, continued briefly in an interim capacity. And when Pastor Shawn and Christina proved their attractiveness, a strong period of growth occurred.

Suddenly new adventures sprang up like wildflowers and the new life promised by our church name was evidenced everywhere.

Paul Tournier wrote a truth in his book, *The Adventure of Living,* paraphrased this way:

"Every adventure of life is doomed to die; some sooner, some later. But out of each death there springs the seeds of a new adventure, similar to the old one, but larger now."

That insight applies to NLCC perfectly. The transition went very well despite dire predictions that Pastor Shawn would be a sacrificial lamb after my long pastorate. The credit is mostly

God's for this smooth change, but Pastor Shawn certainly deserves recognition, too.

He has not been intimidated by my previous leadership and has been a paradigm of graciousness. When my wife asked him if He would have people write cards or letters to me on my 70th birthday, he said he'd certainly do that, but it wasn't enough. He then suggested and directed a 70th birthday party for me at the church that was dubbed by Eugene Peterson as the finest church celebration he had ever witnessed. Shawn was there, speaking, leading, serving...while having a kidney stone attack. Christina cheerfully worked the tables in a servant's white apron.

We could attend the church now and be welcomed at every level. We don't because God wants Karen and me to have new adventures also. We totally cleared out. Churches can experience difficulty at pastoral transitions if the outgoing pastor cannot release control. Vision will be recast, things will be done differently. That church building he helped design and construct will see significant remodeling.

I had seen jealousy and resentment flare in retiring pastors while I served as a presbyter in the Montana District. The leaving pastor wouldn't vacate. He wouldn't clean out his desk. I made a note of that.

"We let go, with a pang, of piece after piece of our lives!"

That sentence, spoken at a Veteran's Day memorial service in 1962 is one I've recalled during my retirement. Releasing my privileged position in Polson has given me a few pangs, but not many! We had our time in the sun. We had our adventures with that church as long as God wished.

We weren't throwing anything away by retiring.

It was just time for relinquishment.

Follow-up Information

- Order autographed book(s) at www.bonmotmedia.com.

- Audiobook, read by author, available soon at www.bonmotmedia.com.

- Ratings, reviews, inside looks and one-click ordering at www.amazon.com.

- A **sequel** is not unthinkable. More stories of value are being written.

- The book is available on KINDLE.

- Author's blog, book-related pictures are on www.milesfinchonline.com.

- Mailing address: Miles Finch, Box 682, Lakeside MT 59922

Author

Miles C. Finch was born in Miles City, Montana in 1938. The last child of twelve born, he moved with his parents to Bigfork, Montana in 1954. After high school, he graduated from Seattle Pacific University in 1960 (B.A. in Psychology) and married his high-school sweetheart, Karen. After the death of their first son, the author attended Fuller Theological seminary (M.Div.), graduating in 1966. He served a student pastorate in Bigfork, Montana, for two years, from 1961 – 1963, and after seminary he pastored only one church, New Life Christian Center in Polson, Montana, for thirty-seven years to the day. He lives now near Lakeside, Montana, where he writes, dabbles at photography, builds rock walls, and enjoys (at a distance) his two children, Kevin and Kimberly (with their spouses Karen and Carmen), and his six grandchildren: Megan, Peter, Brendan, and Kelsey, Cameron and Colby.

Endnotes

1 Psalm 139:15 THE MESSAGE. All references from this translation used with the author's permission.

2 From "God's Message for Each Day", Eugene Peterson, Thomas Nelson (Countryman), 2004, April 1, P. 102

3 Matthew 16:16

4 Matthew 16:22

5 Matthew 5:3 Emphasis mine

6 Hebrews 5:7

7 Acts 2:21

8 I Timothy 6:11

9 I Timothy 6:9

10 Psalms 37:25,26

11 *Letters from the Desert,* by Carlo Carretto. Quoted in "A Guide to Prayer for Ministers and Other Servants", The Upper Room, Nashville, Tenn. P. 146

12 2 Cor. 5:14, THE MESSAGE

13 2 Cor. 5:2-5,9 THE MESSAGE

14 Jane Austin in her novel EMMA.

15 Genesis 12:3, author's paraphrase.

16 Read Numbers 12 for the story about Miriam.

17 This rumor came to me from a dependable and contemporary source. A local man, who as a child fished often with Blossom, questioned this rumor and praised the way she related to all the children on the city dock.

18 James 5:16

19 Mere Christianity, Macmillan, 1978, p. 109

20 Ibid., pp. 112, 113.

21 Proverbs 15:1

22 Matthew 11:28-30

23 Christian Perfection, *Chapter 41 "Humility",* Bethany Fellowship, 1975, paragraph 2, p. 205

24 I Cor. 2:9

25 The most complete biography is GEORGE MULLER OF BRISTOL and His Witness to a Prayer Hearing God, by Arthur T. Pierson, Fleming H. Revell Company

26 Full quote: "It is a common feeling that only the *well-to-do* have a right to be hospitable. The ideal flower of hospitality is almost unknown to the rich; it can hardly be grown save in the gardens of the poor; it is one of their beatitudes." George Macdonald: An Anthology by C.S. Lewis, Macmillan Dolphin Books, 1962, #352, p. 147

27 Hebrews 12:15,16a

28 John 3:19-21

29 Colossians 1:27

30 Revelation 3:20, The MESSAGE

31 James 5:16

32 It is getting more difficult, though. Previously, the major denominations affirmed Biblical theology and based their beliefs and practices on the clear statements of Scripture. Now, with so many church hierarchies rewriting their theology to

cater to prevailing community opinion (or to what they wish would become prevailing opinion,) theological unity is harder to achieve, which makes jovial fellowship more difficult. To some pastors it feels impossible.

33 Matthew 13:24-30, 36-43. For a marvelous treatment of this parable (and other parables) see *The Waiting Father*, Helmut Thielicke, Harper and Row, 1959, pp. 71–82.